The publisher gratefully acknowledges the generous support of the Simpson Humanities Endowment Fund of the University of California Press Foundation.

EVERYONE'S A WINNER

EVERYONE'S A
WINNER

LIFE IN OUR CONGRATULATORY CULTURE

JOEL BEST

UNIVERSITY OF CALIFORNIA PRESS

Berkeley Los Angeles London

University of California Press, one of the most distinguished university presses in the United States, enriches lives around the world by advancing scholarship in the humanities, social sciences, and natural sciences. Its activities are supported by the UC Press Foundation and by philanthropic contributions from individuals and institutions. For more information, visit www.ucpress.edu.

University of California Press
Berkeley and Los Angeles, California

University of California Press, Ltd.
London, England

Portions of chapters 1 and 2 appeared in "Prize Proliferation," *Sociological Forum* 23 (2008): 1–27.

Library of Congress Cataloging-in-Publication Data

Best, Joel.
    Everyone's a winner : life in our congratulatory culture / Joel Best.
        p.   cm.
    Includes bibliographical references and index.
    ISBN 978-0-520-26716-9 (cloth : alk. paper)
    1. Social status—United States.   2. Equality—United States.   3. Motivation (Psychology)—United States.   4. United States—Social life and customs.
5. United States—Social conditions.   I. Title.
    HN90.S6B47   2011
    305—dc22   2010034646

Text: 10.75/15 Janson
Display: Ultramagnetic Light and Regular
Compositor: BookMatters, Berkeley
Printer and binder: Maple-Vail Book Manufacturing Group

Manufactured in the United States of America

20 19 18 17 16 15 14 13 12 11
10 9 8 7 6 5 4 3 2 1

The paper used in this publication meets the minimum requirements of ANSI/NISO Z39.48-1992 (R 1997) (*Permanence of Paper*).

For Ryan

CONTENTS

ACKNOWLEDGMENTS

At various times, Benigno Aguirre, Ronet Bachman, John Barnshaw, Joan Best, Peter Blum, Anne Bowler, Gerald Bracey, Spencer Cahill, Karen Cerulo, Joan DelFattore, Gary Alan Fine, David Grazian, Robert Hampel, Philip Jenkins, Aaron Kupchik, Kathe Lowney, Brian Newby, Larry Nichols, David Schweingruber, and Rhys Williams made helpful comments on various versions of this work.

I also want to thank the people at the University of California Press—especially Naomi Schneider and Dore Brown—for once again shepherding my work into print. Ellen F. Smith, the copyeditor, was especially helpful.

CHAPTER ONE

LIFE IN AN ERA
OF STATUS ABUNDANCE

I live surrounded by excellence. On a drive to our local shopping center, I find myself behind an SUV with a bumper sticker declaring the driver's pride in being the parent of a middle-school honor roll student. In the parking lot, I wind up next to a car bearing a red, white, and blue magnetic ribbon that says, "U.S.A.–#1." Several of the storefronts in the shopping center sport banners or other signs reporting that the stores have received statewide honors. I live in a small state, and I realize that it must be easier to be designated the "Best ___ in Delaware" than it would be elsewhere. Still, these signs tell me that our small shopping center contains a remarkable number of establishments that have been designated as offering outstanding services (our state's best preschool and its best veterinarian) or for selling terrific merchandise (Delaware's best Chinese take-out and burgers). The sandwich shop has a wall *covered* with framed certificates declaring that it has won various awards for serving the state's best cheesesteaks, hoagies, deli, etc., etc. Before the video store closed, it was filled with DVD boxes identifying movies that had received Oscars, film festival awards, or at the least "two thumbs up." At the newsstand, I can find magazines rating the best colleges, hospitals, high schools, employers, places to live, places to retire, and on and on. The party store features an "Award Center" rack with an array of colored ribbons that can be awarded to a "Good Eater," a "Star Singer," or someone who has turned fifty or is having some other birthday evenly divisible by ten. Back home, when I log onto my computer, my university's home page features today's news items, a large share of which report that some professor or student on our campus has won a prize. And so on. Several times each day, I encounter claims that someone has been designated excellent by somebody else.

The fact that some third party has made these designations is key. If I own a pizza parlor and put up a sign declaring that I bake the best pizzas around, most customers will be skeptical of my self-serving claims. But, if after counting the ballots submitted by their readers, *Delaware Today* magazine or the *Wilmington News Journal* newspaper identifies the best pizza in Delaware, that information somehow seems a little more convincing, and a merchant who displays a banner announcing such an award seems to be doing more than just bragging. Somebody else—some third party, whether it's expert judges or just whoever responded to some poll—has vouched for the excellence of this hamburger, that preschool, or whatever.

We pass out praise and superlatives freely. Americans have a global reputation for being full of ourselves. We chant, "U.S.A.—Number One! U.S.A.—Number One!" We confidently describe our country as the world's greatest, its sole superpower. But self-congratulation is far more than a matter of national pride. It is a theme that runs throughout our contemporary society.

The kudos begin early. These days, completing elementary school, kindergarten, even preschool may involve a graduation ceremony, complete with caps and gowns. Many children receive a trophy each time they participate in an organized sports program, beginning with kindergarten soccer or T-ball, so that lots of third graders have already accumulated a dresser-top full of athletic trophies. Many elementary school classrooms anoint a "Student of the Week." Experts justify this praise by arguing that children benefit from encouragement, positive reinforcement, or "warm fuzzies." As the commentator Michael Barone sees it: "From ages six to eighteen Americans live mostly in what I call Soft America—the parts of our country where there is little competition and accountability. . . . Soft America coddles: our schools, seeking to instill self-esteem, ban tag and dodgeball, and promote just about anyone who shows up."[1]

But children aren't the only beneficiaries of our self-congratulatory culture. Awards, prizes, and honors go to adults—and to companies, communities, and other organizations—in ever-increasing numbers. It is remarkable how much of our news coverage concerns Nobel Prizes, Academy Awards, and other designations of excellence. And, at the end of life, obituaries often highlight the deceased's honors ("Bancroft Dies at 73. Won Oscar, Emmy, Tony"). Congratulatory culture extends nearly from the cradle to the grave.

This isn't how we like to think of ourselves. Michael Barone insists: "From ages eighteen to thirty Americans live mostly in Hard America—the parts of American life subject to competition and accountability. . . . Hard America plays for keeps: the private sector fires people when profits fall, and the military trains under live fire."[2] The imagined world of Hard America is governed by impersonal market forces, and rewards don't come easily. There is stiff competition, and only the best survive and thrive. This vision begins American history with no-nonsense Puritans whose God expected them to work hard and receive their rewards in heaven. People were to live steady lives and gain the quiet admiration of others for their steadfast characters. Pride was one of the seven deadly sins. In this view, our contemporary readiness to praise—and to celebrate our own (or at least our middle schoolers') accomplishments—seems to be something new.

So what's going on? Why are contemporary Americans so ready to pass out prizes and congratulate one another on their wonderfulness? What are the consequences of this self-congratulatory culture? This book attempts to answer these broad questions by focusing on a few specific, yet telling, developments. It examines the trend toward awarding ever more prizes, as well as our schools' struggles to define excellence. More generally, it looks at changes in the way Americans think about heroism, and at the causes and consequences of our eagerness to rate and rank.

First, however, we need to take a step back. Awards, prizes, and honors are forms of what sociologists call social status, and we need to begin by considering how status works.

SOCIAL STATUS

The great German sociologist Max Weber argued that societies rank their members along economic, political, and social dimensions. We usually think of economic rankings in terms of *class;* belonging to a higher class means that you have more money, higher income, or greater wealth than those in lower classes. Similarly, political rankings involve differences in *power*—the degree to which you can compel others to do what you want them to do. Social rankings, the third dimension, concern *status*—how much prestige, esteem, respect, or honor one receives from others.[3]

For the most part, social scientists act as though class and power are more important than status. They write far, far more books and articles about class and power—and about race and gender, which also have come to be viewed as key bases for ranking people in our society—than about status. Class, power, race, and gender are treated as serious matters, and each receives extensive coverage even in introductory sociology textbooks. In contrast, status seems to be considered slightly silly, and it attracts far less attention from analysts and textbook authors. For most people, the word "status" brings to mind *status symbols*— vain people driving fancy cars or wearing ostentatious jewelry in hopes of impressing others. It is easy to dismiss such bling—rappers sporting saucer-sized, bejeweled medallions and the like— as unimportant.

But this ignores the central role status plays in our everyday lives. Oh, most of us may not go around flaunting pricey material goods, but we care—a lot—about whether others respect us. We think it is important to be well regarded. In extreme cases, status can become a matter of life and death. Think of inner-city homicides that start with one youth "dissing" (disrespecting) another; or think of duels between high-born gentlemen over points of honor. Those are lethal arguments about status.

But status concerns aren't limited to gangbangers and argumentative aristocrats. Most of us want to be well regarded by other people, and we try to behave in ways that will earn their respect. At least in the short run, there isn't much most of us can do to alter our social class or our power—let alone our race or gender—but we can always bid for more respect, for higher status. When we meet someone for the first time, we try to make a good first impression. When we go on a job interview, we show up clean, well groomed, neatly dressed, and speaking politely. When we say "please" and "thank you," we are demonstrating that we know how to observe the rituals of politeness. All of these efforts to make the best impression are attempts to gain others' respect, little moves in the everyday status games that we all play.

And we are sensitive to how others treat us. Are they according us the proper amount of respect? Or do they somehow convey that they look down on us, that they aren't that favorably impressed? Across time and space, we can find examples of societies where status differences were blatant. Feudal nobles could beat their vassals, and those vassals could not raise a hand in response. In the segregated South, there were countless ways of affirming the gulf in racial status: African-Americans were supposed to step aside, to use polite titles to address whites ("Mr. Strom"), while whites could call blacks by their first names, and so on. From our contemporary vantage point, such imbalanced status rituals strike us as wrong.

Our society operates along more democratic principles. Today's etiquette demands that all people receive a minimum level of courteous treatment, so that under ordinary circumstances we grant everyone some ritual respect. Of course, this hardly means that we all have the same status. Displaying a certain degree of courtesy to everyone is merely one of the most basic moves in the contemporary American status game. As we will see, things quickly get more complex.

American sociologists have tended to conflate status and class. They speak of "socio-economic status" (SES), and much of their research on status concerns occupational prestige (basically surveys used to rank the status of different occupations—studies showing that heart surgeons are looked up to more than bootblacks). In this view, class and status are closely correlated. No wonder that we tend to equate status symbols with expensive material goods; people who have lots of money can afford to spend it on fancy cars and expensive jewelry as way of displaying their wealth.[4]

But there are two problems with conflating status and class. First, we need to realize that status symbols are not limited to expensive trinkets. There are all sorts of nonmaterial status symbols. Parents who correct their children's grammar ("Don't say 'Me and Jim,' say 'Jim and I'") or try to supervise their clothing and grooming choices are teaching status lessons. One's word choices, clothing, and grooming convey information about one's status. There are all sorts of status symbols that don't cost a dime (although they may require consciously learning what to do and how to do it). We can tell a lot about people's social class by listening to them talk (What do they choose to talk about? Which words do they choose? What sort of accent do they have?) or observing them in social situations (How do they behave?). A standard theme in social comedies is the person whose material and nonmaterial status symbols don't tell the same story: the newly rich individual who can afford to live in a mansion but doesn't observe upper-class customs (think *The Beverly Hillbillies*); or the former aristocrat fallen on hard times who struggles to maintain a proud pose even in debased circumstances (such as the socialite turned soldier in *Private Benjamin*). Money can buy some status symbols, but not all.[5]

The second problem is that, while social class and occupation certainly involve status, so do aspects of social life far removed from economic life. Max Weber coined another important concept—lifestyle. He recognized that people belonged to all sorts of social groupings, and those groups had their own systems for allocating status and for making status claims. To understand lifestyle, imagine a suburban high school where all of the students come from middle-class homes. Even though a sociologist would classify them as members of the same social class, students within that high school are able to choose their place in the school's social system. Some will become heavily involved in athletics, others in academics, still others in social life, or rebellion, or whatever. That is, within the school setting, the students—who, remember, all come from middle-class families—can come to think of themselves and be considered by others to be very different sorts of people—jocks, nerds, stoners, whatever. Each of these identities comes with a lifestyle; that is, the members of each group tend to favor particular clothing and hairstyles, musical tastes, and patterns for alcohol and drug use, so that it is fairly easy for anyone familiar with the local status symbols to classify individuals into their different lifestyle groups. The distinctions between these categories aren't rigid; some talented athletes are excellent students, and so on. Yet each group assigns respect—status—to its members based on its own criteria for excellence, and everyone knows that the groups enjoy different relative status within the school as a whole.[6]

Adults can choose among far more status groupings, each with its associated lifestyle. Certainly class/money plays a role, but so do other factors—ethnicity, religion, age, education, hobbies, and so on. There are, for instance, lots of different middle-class lifestyles. What—if anything—you read or watch on television, what you eat, how you spend your free time, how you raise your children, and countless other choices reflect, not just your social class, but the particular status groups to which you belong.[7]

SOCIAL WORLDS

Society, then, is composed of many small groups within which members assign and receive status. Sociologists disagree about the best name for these groupings; different terms emphasize different aspects of these groups. Calling them *status groups* plays up—and arguably exaggerates—the importance of status (the journalist Tom Wolfe coined the term *statusspheres,* which has the same quality). Another possibility is to speak of *subcultures* (which emphasizes each group's distinctive culture, its values and beliefs). Other sociologists favor *scenes* (a term that highlights social geography, the places where different groups congregate), *fields* (a concept that envisions social spaces where people compete for resources), or *tribes* or even *neo-tribes* (terms used to characterize heterogeneous groups that draw members from many different classes). Still another option—the one I prefer—is to speak of these groups as *social worlds,* a term that reminds us how people can become immersed—live much of their lives—within particular social groups.[8]

Each social world judges its members—that is, assigns them status—according to its own criteria. Often, the members' standards may strike people outside that social world as peculiar. Consider, for example, Civil War reenactors—those folks who wear Confederate or Union uniforms and meet to camp out, drill, and reenact battles. Reenacting is a hobby—something people do for fun—but it is also an elaborate social world that has its own organizations, magazines, websites, merchants, and so forth. In fact, there are significant social divisions within the reenacting world. Because reenactors seek to duplicate something of the past, many of them become concerned with historical authenticity, and over time their standards for what should be considered authentic have risen. Where once reenactors might have purchased outfits made with modern fabrics, the more serious reenactors came to insist on more authentic cloth, assembled in more authentic ways. What might strike outsiders as trivial details—the nature of the buttons used, or the way the buttonholes were sewn—became ways of judging one's commitment to the reenactment project, symbols of status within the reenacting world. Of course, wearing authentic clothing is both more expensive and less comfortable, and the reenacting world has faced tensions between those deeply committed to authenticity (who describe themselves as "hardcore") and those more concerned with enjoying the fun of reenacting than with achieving authenticity (dismissed by the hardcore reenactors as "farbs"). Hardcore reenactors try to distance themselves from farbs, so that what seems at first glance to be a single reenacting world can actually be subdivided into more-or-less distinct hardcore and farb worlds.[9]

Very similar tensions characterize the social world of barbershop quartets, where those committed to the traditional barbershop repertoire have found themselves in conflict with modernizers, who want to sing more contemporary songs and introduce various stylistic innovations. In this case, the traditionalists (known as "kibbers," for "keep it barbershop") tend to be older than the modernizers; they warn against the "dangers of musical sophistication" and argue that modernization "emasculates" barbershop music. After the modernizers took control of the Barbershop Harmony Society, the pastime's leading organization, traditionalists broke away to form their own Barbershop Quartet Preservation Association.[10]

For those of us who are neither reenactors nor barbershop singers, these struggles may seem strange. What does it matter whether a reenactor's uniform has buttons manufactured using traditional methods or whether a barbershop quartet wants to sing Beach Boys songs? But for members of those worlds these can become key status issues, determining who will and won't receive respect within that world. And, when a world's members cannot agree, the world often splits in two, so that separate worlds emerge—each with its own group, lifestyle, and status standards.

This process of division is fundamental and can be seen in all sorts of social worlds: a set of businesses come to define themselves as distinct and establish their own trade association, trade magazines, and so on; a group of researchers decide to organize their own scholarly society and publish their own journal to report work in their specialty; musicians who like to play in a particular style establish their own musical genre; and so on. In each of these cases, people who share a set of interests come to feel that they cannot get the respect they deserve in the larger, existing social world, and they find advantages in setting up a league of their own, a separate world where they can recognize and reward what they view as appropriate behavior. Status concerns, then, are central to the establishment of these new social worlds.[11]

Recognizing the way that new social worlds are constantly being created in our society forces us to rethink some of sociologists' most basic assumptions about status. Their tendency to link status to the enduring edifice of social class ignores the relative ease with which status standards can be created and changed. It can be fairly difficult for individuals to move from one class to another; in contrast, the creation of new social worlds makes it quite easy for people to join new status systems. Employees who may look ahead to years in the same job with minimal opportunities to advance in social class find fewer obstacles to, say, becoming—and gaining status as—a hardcore Civil War reenactor. Status is more fluid, more easily changed than class or power.

This relates to a second assumption that underpins sociologists' thinking about status: that is, that status—like money or power—is a scarce resource. Many analysts assume that there is a limited amount of status, less than enough to go around. Its scarcity is what makes status valuable, so that people compete to gain status. If one person gains prestige, the thinking goes, it is to some degree at the expense of others. Some of the leading discussions of status involve quasi-economic reasoning, arguing that market mechanisms govern the allocation of prestige.[12] Certainly, many people want more status, just as they want more money. In that sense, there will always be less status than people desire. The perceived shortage of status—insufficient respect being given to people like us—is one of the reasons disenchanted people form new social worlds. But the ability to establish a new social world means that folks aren't forced to spend their whole lives in circles where they inevitably lose in the competition for status. Rather, by creating their own worlds, they acquire the ability to mint status of their own. They can decide who deserves respect and why.

This process is one of the reasons that we live in a time of status abundance. Commentators have described post–World War II Americans as living in an affluent society, that is, in an era when many people enjoy very high standards of living, with large proportions of the population owning their own homes, cars, and so on.[13] This is economic affluence. In much the same way, we can think of contemporary America as experiencing an era of status affluence, when there are far more opportunities to gain status than in the past. As the commentator David Brooks notes: "Everybody gets to be an aristocrat now. And the number of social structures is infinite.... In this segmented world everybody gets to be successful."[14]

Of course people continue to desire more status, just as the economically affluent want more money, but the relative abundance of status is changing how we live.

STATUS AFFLUENCE

Even under conditions of status affluence, people continue to act as though status is in short supply. The proud parents who display a bumper sticker announcing that their child is a middle-school honor roll student are declaring that their kid is an especially good student. Presumably, only some—not all—of the students at that middle school are on the honor roll. If every student in the school was to be designated an "honor roll student," then the honor might seem meaningless. Similarly, when we see a banner announcing that this shop's sandwiches have been rated tops in Delaware, we assume that other places serving sandwiches didn't get that coveted top rating. Status depends upon making distinctions between those who deserve more respect and those who merit less.

Status affluence doesn't mean that everyone is of exactly equal status. Rather, it means that there are lots of opportunities to gain status, and those opportunities are increasing. The *Wilmington News Journal* only began polling readers to determine which preschool or Chinese take-out was considered the state's best about twenty years ago. When these rankings began, a whole new category of status came into being (and, over the years, the number of categories covered by the newspaper's polls increased, and *Delaware Today* magazine began running its own poll, so that the total number of "Best in Delaware" awards has grown and grown). Similarly, even if middle schools have placed students on honor rolls for some time, the practice of giving the students' parents bumper stickers began more recently. There are many signs that there is a lot more status to go around in today's self-congratulatory culture. What accounts for this development?

Status affluence is the result of three trends that character-ized American society during the decades following World War II. During the long Great Depression that preceded that war, American society was characterized by scarcity: too many people had too little money, let alone status. The war put people back to work, but wartime rationing kept them from indulging themselves. However, the war's end launched a prolonged period of prosperity: standards of living rose as people bought houses in the suburbs and filled them with televisions and other con-sumer goods. This economic affluence, in turn, fostered three enduring social trends that continue to support status affluence: first, people could afford to join—and could choose among—a growing number of social worlds; second, they also had more resources—more money, but also more leisure time and better information—to support those choices; and, third, those choices could be justified in multiple ways. These developments—more status-generating groups, more resources to support the groups' activities, and more ways to justify awarding status—created the conditions that allow status affluence to flourish.

1. The Growing Number of Groups Allocating Status

There is a sense in which most status is local.[15] Even small social groupings assign some members more prestige than others; any group of young boys has its leader. These localized status rankings often go unstated—individuals look up to others without there being any sort of formal or even articulated ranking. But sometimes there are steps at formalization: the group names itself; perhaps it specifies leadership roles or offices and formally designates individuals to fill those positions; there may be a set of rules devised to govern the members' behavior. Even delinquent gangs sometimes adopt such formal trappings, as do all manner of more respectable clubs and other voluntary associations.

While it may be possible to live a life completely outside such formalized arrangements and remain totally within an informal world of family and friends, it is becoming less likely. Today's parents "sign up" their children for soccer leagues and T-ball teams, band, Scouting, and so on.[16] High school students join athletic teams, the yearbook staff, orchestra, French Club, and other organized activities. As adults, people become members of religious congregations, officers in the PTA or their homeowners' association, or whatever. And, at every age group, local groups may have formal ties to citywide, statewide, even national organizations.[17]

All of these groups, simply by designating leadership roles, allocate a degree of status among their members. Note their diversity: these groups vary according to their members' race, class, gender, sexual orientation, occupation, ideology, religion, and all manner of other dimensions. It makes no difference: all sorts of people allocate status. But that is hardly the end of the matter. Some groups grow, and their organization tends to become more elaborate, with more officially designated positions that bring status to individuals. Often, the group sanctions more-or-less friendly competition: a kindergarten soccer league has a schedule of games, as do the teams in an adult slow-pitch softball league. Some people do well in these competitions and thereby earn more status. The group may also award prizes to those who embody whatever values the group considers important—yet another form of status. Over time, a group tends to evolve in ways that increase the number of people who derive status from the group. And, to the degree that this evolution improves the group's ability to communicate to both its members and those outside the group via such means as a newsletter or a website, information about the group's status attributions is likely to come to the attention of a growing number of people. Often, these developments pay off: the group's stature, its economic position, even its political influence may swell, reinforcing the links among status, class, and power.

Moreover, as we have seen in our discussion of social worlds, there is always the possibility that those members of a group who feel left out or underappreciated can split off and form their own group—a league of their own based on their vision of authentic reenacting or barbershopping or whatever. Each of those new groups becomes a new factory for manufacturing status. In short, the first cause of increased status affluence is the proliferation of groups within contemporary society, because each group becomes a source for the creation of additional status.

2. Increased Resources for Status Creation

The increasing number of status-producing groups reflects the greater availability of resources needed to create and maintain such groups. Most obviously, economic affluence fosters status creation by generating *discretionary income,* so that after they cover their basic living expenses, individuals have money left over that they can choose to spend in different ways. To the degree that participation in hardcore reenacting and other social worlds costs money (and some reenactors purchase thousands of dollars' worth of gear), individuals can afford those costs. Affluence does not mean that every member of society can join just any social world; relatively few of us can afford to mingle among people who own large yachts. Still, most people find they have a choice of lifestyles available to individuals with about their amount of discretionary income.

This lifestyle diversity is supported by the media and merchants that serve particular social worlds. Immediately after World War II, many intellectuals worried about the emergence of mass society—a society in which individuals would be alienated members of a great undifferentiated mass that received the same messages from centralized mass media.[18] This Orwellian vision failed to materialize, because society was never a homogeneous mass; as we have already noted, society contains many social worlds, each with its own lifestyle and status system, and these are continually subdividing into ever more social worlds. Similarly, mass media—in the sense of media that sought to reach the great mass, *all* of society's members—proved to be a poor business model.

In one medium after another—movies, magazines, even eventually television—it became clear that it was more profitable to address specific, segmented audiences, defined by sex, age, ethnicity, lifestyle, and so on, rather than trying to capture and hold the attention of the mass. Thus, weekly general-interest magazines, such as *Life, Look,* and the *Saturday Evening Post,* became unprofitable precisely because they attracted huge numbers of diverse readers each week; advertisers found it was too expensive to reach the mass audience that read those magazines because most products tend to be purchased by particular sorts of people, and it was more efficient to advertise in magazines with smaller circulations, so long as their readers were concentrated in the demographic groups that offered the most likely customers. A glance at today's newsstands reveals that contemporary magazines target very specific groups of readers, whose interests often focus on particular lifestyle concerns. Such targeted media not only are more profitable but encourage membership in particular social worlds by keeping individuals apprised of those worlds' developments and status systems. And, of course, the Internet and other technological innovations have made it far easier for individuals with shared interests to contact one another, thereby fostering both the survival of existing social worlds and the possibility of creating new ones.[19]

The same process is replicated in our shopping malls, where most vendors are branches of national chains calculated to serve particular lifestyles. Thus, adolescents can shop in Hot Topic for punk merchandise, or Pacific Sunwear for skater/surfer styles, and so on. Consumer affluence leads to a consumption-centered economy in which media address segmented audiences in order to attract merchants who hope to sell to those markets. A visit to any supermarket reveals commercialized diversity: Coca-Cola is now Classic Coke, just one of an array of Cokes, sugared and diet, caffeinated or not, flavored with lemon, cherry, vanilla, and so on; just as Crest toothpaste is available in multiple flavors with various health and beauty additives. These consumer choices allow people in different social worlds to equip themselves differently and, in the process, display their engagement in distinctive lifestyles.[20]

There is a long intellectual tradition denouncing these developments and arguing that people cannot find authentic meaning in the pursuit of consumer goods associated with different lifestyles. Perhaps not, but economic affluence certainly supports people's efforts to establish distinct social worlds and thereby fosters the growth of status—and the attendant status symbols—associated with different lifestyles and social worlds.

In addition to economic affluence, time and information are key resources in fostering the expansion of status. Contemporary society is awash in news; it has never been easier to gather or spread information. Modern technologies link most American households to dozens, even hundreds of cable and satellite television networks, to the Internet, to e-mail, and to ever fancier phones. Greater amounts of information travel farther and faster than ever before, and this means that it is easier to learn about status—and a remarkably large share of news communicates information about status. Some of this information interests very large audiences, such as the folks who follow the status contests televised on *Survivor* or *American Idol,* but much of it is interpersonal, such as gossipy text-messages or e-mail sent to friends. And, of course, it helps that people have enough free time to stay on top of at least some of the current shifts in status. We live in a society where many people have enough money, information, and time to pay attention to status concerns.

3. Multiple Popular Justifications for Awarding More Status

Within each social world, status is a claim of distinction, of relative superiority. Each world's members say, in effect: "Our way represents a better way of reenacting [or barbershopping or whatever]; other ways are inferior." When sociologists analyze status, they often fix on these claims of distinction; further, they argue that, to the degree lifestyles require money or other scarce resources, status reinforces class differences. That is, people with more money are often able to command more status and look down on those of lower class and, therefore, lesser status.[21]

However, our society celebrates, not just distinction, but democracy and equality. While we might imagine that these values would translate into a suspicion of status as anti-egalitarian, they actually serve to support the expansion of status. Instead of leading to proposals to eliminate status distinctions, the recognition that some people have higher status than others often leads to calls for leveling, for awarding more status for those currently receiving less recognition. It is usually difficult to convince a social world that is already awarding status to stop doing so, particularly if those calling for reform do not belong to that world. Such outsiders lack much influence within the group. For one thing, they lack status within the world they're criticizing, and it is often easy for a world's members to discount their critics as motivated by sour grapes. In contrast, it usually is much easier to convince those currently cut off from a group's respect that they, too, deserve to gain status. If nothing else works, they can break off into a new social world where they can establish their own status system.

For instance, if a university honors professors who make noteworthy contributions, and if someone notices that the winners tend to be white males, it is easy to suggest that there ought to be one or more special awards for outstanding female or non-white faculty. That is, groups that find themselves disadvantaged in existing status competitions may establish their own competitions that their members can win. It is easy to justify this as a way of celebrating the many different sorts of excellence in different groups. And, of course, the growing number of social worlds means that newer groups are particularly likely to feel that they need to allocate status to their members, so as to make participation in their world as rewarding as involvement in established groups.

There are several justifications for expanding the supply of status—beyond straightforward claims that members of other groups are receiving status, and therefore our members ought to receive status, too. For instance, status often opens doors that allow people to get ahead. High school students who have distinguished themselves (by, say, winning competitions for musical proficiency or whatever) improve their prospects of gaining admission to more selective colleges. Therefore, increasing the number of ways students can gain such distinctions raises the number of students whose chances for admission can be improved. Note that it is not just the individual who stands to gain. The high school wants as many of its students to do as well as possible; if a high school sends its students to selective colleges, that speaks well of the school. Therefore, a high school that offers students many arenas for exhibiting excellence (such as academics, athletic teams, musical programs, clubs, and on so) gives them more chances to gain status, and thereby helps launch them into desirable slots in the larger world, in the process cementing its own reputation as an excellent school.

There is also the assumption that status recognition will inspire those who receive it. This is particularly true when people talk about children and adolescents. Our culture no longer subscribes to the notion that beatings are the best way to encourage good behavior by the young. Rather, we emphasize the importance of rewards—of positive reinforcements. For example, DARE—the most popular drug education program, usually taught around fifth grade—involves classroom sessions, followed by a ceremony marking the students' new status as trained drug resistors. DARE graduates receive various trinkets—T-shirts, plastic wristbands featuring anti-drug slogans, or school supplies bearing the DARE logo—presumably on the theory that these will serve as status symbols and reminders of the program's message.

Providing status enhancements to the young is also one way of enhancing self-esteem, one of the key pop-psychology concepts in recent decades. Its advocates argue that most social ills are rooted in people's failure to think sufficiently well of themselves. Why do some kids use drugs? They have low self-esteem. Why do some teenagers get pregnant? Same answer. You get the idea. If low self-esteem is at the root of most social problems, the argument goes, we might inoculate young people against those problems by enhancing their self-esteem. And one way to encourage people to think better of themselves is to tell them that they are well regarded by others. Thus, advocates argue, enhancing people's status can be an important force for social good.[22]

One of the key patterns in social life is that advantages tend to be cumulative. Students from higher-income homes tend to receive higher grades in school—probably for all sorts of reasons (e.g., their parents tend to be better educated and to emphasize the value of education, their families tend to be more stable, and so on). Those high-income, good-grade students tend to get more than their share of the status rewards their schools offer. But, the self-esteem argument goes, it is the low-income, low-status kids who could really benefit from status enhancements; they are the ones who, if only they felt better about themselves, might be steered away from drugs, dropping out, and other social problems. Since most of these students lack the advantages of their high-income classmates in the competition for good grades, other sorts of status need to be made available to recognize their worth and improve their self-esteem.

We have already noted that social worlds tend to create status recognition for their members so that, as the number of social worlds grows, the amount of status also rises. This process is complemented by a range of ideological justifications for adding status rewards. Thus, there may be calls to recognize excellence, to single out those who perform especially well. But rewarding one form of excellence invites other, democratizing justifications for allocating additional status. Aren't there other sorts of excellence that also deserve recognition? And shouldn't we also encourage those who have not achieved excellence to do better? Shouldn't status be allocated so as to rectify inequalities, enhance self-esteem, and so on? The range of ideological rationales for awarding status, like the diversity of social worlds in which status can be earned, encourage expanding the overall amount of status.

Note, too, that establishing a new social world with its attendant status system allows further claims of distinction. Each world is able to declare its own superiority. As David Brooks observes: "[In] this country . . . , everybody can kick everybody else's ass. The crunchies who hike look down on the hunters who squat in the forest downing beers, and the hunters look down on the hikers who perch on logs smoking dope. . . . Nobody in this decentralized, fluid structure knows who is mainstream and who is alternative, who is elite and who is populist."[23] So long as each world's members talk chiefly among themselves, its status can be valued.

Status abundance goes unnoticed precisely because we tend to focus on status within particular worlds rather than on the total supply of status throughout society.[24] Every world's members are likely to agree that some people within that world deserve respect, recognition, and appreciation for their accomplishments and contributions. Gaining such status recognition seems special, a mark of distinction. The implication is that not everyone attains this status. Within a particular world's confines, status may seem rare and valuable. But, when we step back enough so that we can see society as a whole, we discover that supposedly special marks of status are becoming increasingly widespread. Is it possible that the trend toward status affluence cheapens the value of these marks of status?

STATUS INFLATION

We have already noted some ways in which status resembles money. Both are scarce resources, although we live in a period of both economic and status affluence. And, just as economists worry about monetary inflation, there are critics who argue that status, like money, is vulnerable to inflation.[25]

Because contemporary society makes it very easy to manufacture status, so that more people receive more status than in the past, the overall supply of status is growing. But this means, the critics of status affluence argue, that status is less scarce than it once was and, because it is less scarce, it is therefore less valuable. If a high school that used to single out the graduating student with the highest grade point average to be its valedictorian now designates dozens of valedictorians in each graduating class, then, these critics insist, the prestige of being named valedictorian—the value of the status associated with the honor—has to be diminished. Just as printing millions of new dollar bills leads to economic inflation—that is, increasing the supply of money leads to higher prices, so that a dollar buys less than it used to—so increasing the supply of status (by, say, naming more valedictorians) causes status inflation.

Critics of status inflation worry about the causes of status affluence, that is, the reasons that the supply of status has been increasing in contemporary America. They resist efforts to distribute more awards by warning that this only makes the various honors worth less. They complain that when once-rare distinctions become more common, they don't mean as much as they once did. They sneer at the status grubbing apparent in other social worlds, where honors seem to be distributed too widely. Thus, members of one branch of the military will deride a rival service's tendency to award medals for what seem to be marginal accomplishments, or Phi Beta Kappa faculty at one college, who carefully limit the percentage of students on their campus who are admitted to the elite honor society, complain about the PBK chapter at a nearby college rumored to admit a higher proportion of its students.

Such complaints don't seem to do much good. Oh, it may be possible for critics to set firm limits on the amount of status awarded within some particular social world that they control ("On our campus, no more than X percent of students will be admitted to Phi Beta Kappa!"). But those critics' voices have very little effect on status-awarding practices in other social worlds; they cannot control others' decisions to manufacture more status. In particular, those who try to fight status inflation risk accusations that they are haves who seek to block the status opportunities of have-nots ("Those critics don't want folks in our group to get the sorts of recognition people in their group are already getting."). The critics may be able to convince themselves that their own world's honors have not been debased and retain their original high value ("At our high school, there can be only one valedictorian, so that the honor really means something."). But the larger society probably doesn't keep track of the distinctions between social worlds; most people are likely to assume that a valedictorian is a valedictorian, that a medal awarded by one armed service (or a Phi Beta Kappa key from one college) is equivalent to similar awards from other social worlds.

This means that status inflation is likely to continue, and not only because other social worlds will—for all of the reasons discussed in the previous section—be quite willing to honor more of their members. Even within social worlds where people agree that status inflation is a danger, there may be the sense that our world's members will be disadvantaged in the larger society if the honors produced by other social worlds are not recognized as debased. One country's central bank can pursue anti-inflationary monetary policies, reasonably confident that the larger market should adjust exchange rates so that its uninflated currency will become worth more than the debased currency of a neighboring country that allows inflation in its economy. But there are no central markets regulating the relative value of different types of status. Rather, the larger society is unlikely to carefully weigh the value of honors in different social worlds—it is likely to consider all valedictorians or Phi Beta Kappa members equal. And if that's the case, we only hurt our social world's members if we limit status while other social worlds manufacture it more freely. The difficulty of achieving general agreement to limit the production of status makes status inflation highly likely.

Moreover, because there are often ideological justifications—democratization, self-esteem, and so on—for increasing the amount of status, critics who warn about status inflation are vulnerable to charges that they are elitists, people who already have easy access to existing status awards, and therefore a vested interest in limiting others' opportunities for those benefits. They are too easily portrayed as spoilsports, already well positioned at the status trough, who seek to block disadvantaged others' opportunities to achieve recognition. The result? Even when status inflation's critics retain firm control within their own social worlds, they are likely to have far less influence in other social worlds, where they can be criticized for failing to acknowledge the real contributions of other sorts of folks.

SELF-CONGRATULATORY CULTURE

I began this chapter by noting the frequency with which announcements of awards and high rankings occur in contemporary American life. And I have tried to argue that social developments in contemporary American society—including greater economic affluence, the increased availability of leisure time, improved communication, the creation of independent social worlds, and the availability of multiple supportive ideologies—foster the expansion of status, so that more status is being awarded to more people for more reasons and warnings of status inflation tend to be ineffective.

The point is not that the trend toward increasing status is good or bad, but that it has been largely unrecognized. Critics occasionally grumble about this or that instance of status inflation, but the larger phenomenon—growing status affluence—has not received much attention. This book is my effort to describe how and why status is increasing and to assess the consequences of this development.

Are these developments unique to the United States? Is there something about American character, our culture, or our institutions that encourages making status more abundant? Or are these developments found in other countries? Because I am an American sociologist who is most familiar with what's been happening in my own country, I have written a book that concentrates on developments in the United States. However, there are indications that similar processes are in fact occurring elsewhere. When I have talked about this topic with sociologists in Canada, Japan, and Western Europe, they've acknowledged that they see parallels in their own societies, and some of the studies that I cite refer to developments elsewhere. I suspect that self-congratulatory culture may be particularly well developed in the United States, but that other countries don't lag far behind.

The remaining chapters of this book focus on specific aspects of this self-congratulatory culture. Chapter 2 examines the trend toward prize proliferation—the general increase in awards and honors. Chapter 3 explores the dynamics of self-congratulation within schools and higher education. Chapter 4 considers our increased readiness to identify heroes. And chapter 5 looks at the spread of rankings and ratings. Finally, the concluding chapter considers the consequences and the larger significance of these developments.

CHAPTER TWO

PRIZE PROLIFERATION

"Everybody has won, and all must have prizes."
The Dodo; Lewis Carroll,
Alice in Wonderland

In 1946, the Mystery Writers of America (MWA) began awarding Edgar Awards (named for Edgar Allan Poe); these seem to have been the first annual prizes for outstanding mystery or detective fiction. Britain's Crime Writers' Association (CWA) began offering its own awards in 1955. (Their initial prize, the Crossed Red Herrings Award for the best mystery novel, was renamed the Golden Dagger in 1960.) Today, the award programs for both the MWA and the CWA are more than fifty years old, and both have expanded a good deal during that period. In both cases, the categories for which awards are given have shifted but generally increased. For example, the MWA had only four Edgar categories in 1946, but currently awards Edgars in twelve categories, as well as five other special achievement awards. (Meanwhile, other Edgar awards—e.g., Best Radio Drama, one of the original categories—have been dropped.) As late as 1968, the CWA had only a single award, but then a Silver Dagger (for the runner-up) was added in 1969, and the CWA now presents about a dozen awards, including one for lifetime achievement and prizes for the best thriller, the best historical mystery, and so on.[1]

More recently, other annual mystery awards have appeared. These include the Nero Wolfe Award (presented by the Wolfe Pack, a society of fans of that detective; begun in 1979—three categories in recent years); the Shamus Awards (Private Eye Writers of America; begun in 1982—six categories in recent years); the Macavity Awards (Mystery Readers International; begun in 1987—four categories); the Agatha Awards (Malice Domestic, a Washington, D.C., fan organization; begun in 1989—five categories); the Anthony Awards (Bouchercon World Mystery, a major fan convention; begun in 1989—five categories); the Hammett Award (North American Branch of the International Association of Crime Writers; begun in 1992—one category); and the Derringer Awards (Short Mystery Fiction Society; begun in 1997—four categories). There are others. Figure 1 documents the growth in the number of U.S. and U.K. mystery prizes. (The figure does not include awards from other English-speaking countries, such as Canada's Arthur Ellis Awards [seven categories, since 1984] or Australia's Ned Kelly Awards [four categories, since 1996].)[2]

Obviously, there has been a striking increase in the annual number of awards for outstanding mystery fiction. As late as 1985, there were no more than twenty-five prizes awarded each year, whereas in recent years, the total has been about four times that number. Moreover, this is hardly an atypical example. Other popular fiction genres, such as science fiction and romance novels, display the same pattern—a marked increase in the number of prizes in recent decades. The same pattern exists for scholarly books; within my discipline of sociology, for example, the number of prizes given each year for excellent books has grown

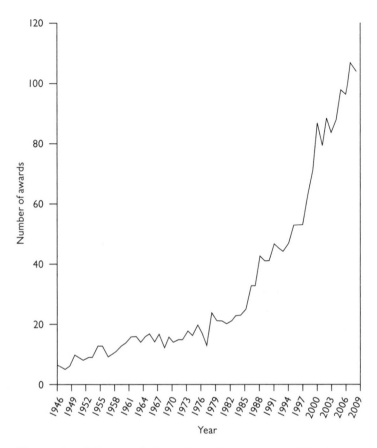

Figure 1. Awards for mysteries in the United States and United Kingdom, 1946–2008.

from one in 1956 to fourteen in 1989 to more than fifty today. Nor is the trend confined to book awards. The number of film prizes awarded worldwide has grown to the point that there are now nearly twice as many awards as there are full-length movies produced. For both books and films, the number of prizes has grown at a far faster clip than the numbers of new books or movies.[3]

Or take major league baseball. Although it has been a well-established institution for many decades, it has seen a similar pattern of increasing numbers of awards for players. For a long time this was a gradual trend: the Cy Young Award honoring the game's best pitcher began in 1956, but since 1967 each league has had its own Cy Young winner; similarly, there was one Rookie of the Year in 1947, but one for each league beginning in 1949. But during the twenty-first century, awards have multiplied at a rapid clip: 2001 introduced the Rookie of the Month Award (really twelve awards, one for each league for each of the six months of the regular season); 2002 brought the This Year in Baseball Awards (online voting by fans for about ten awards); 2003 started the Player of the Week Awards (more than fifty awards each season: twenty-five weeks times two leagues, with frequent ties); 2005 offered several new prizes—the Comeback Player of the Year Award (two—one for each league), the Delivery Man of the Month Award (six awards per season), and the Delivery Man of the Year Award (one award each year); while 2007 added prizes for the Clutch Performer of the Month (six awards) and the Clutch Performer of the Year (one award). That's around ninety new awards added in a decade for a sport in which awards were already fairly plentiful—for instance, each league has awarded nine Gold Glove Awards, one for each position, since 1957, as well as nine Silver Slugger Awards since 1980.[4]

And we see the same process at work in all sorts of other social sectors. Universities are awarding more honorary degrees than ever before. The number of medals presented to members of the Marine Corps increased during the peacetime interval between Vietnam and the Gulf War. The Army displays a similar pattern: "In 1988, one in four soldiers was recognized for distinguished achievement or service by receiving a Legion of Merit, Meritorious Service Medal, Army Commendation Medal or Army Achievement Medal. Ten years later: one in every 2.2 soldiers." In 1985, the Iowa State Fair held cooking contests in 25 divisions; less than twenty years later, there were 168 divisions, which were further subdivided into about nine hundred classes (each of which awarded a blue ribbon for the best dish). The number of college football bowl games grew from twenty-three at the end of the 1999 season to thirty-four ten years later, enough so that more than half of the teams in the top division could play in a bowl game. And, of course, many parents have experienced "trophy creep"—the practice of having ever-younger children bringing home athletic trophies awarded for participation on a team. Nor is the trend restricted to the United States; for instance, recent decades saw a rapid growth in Malaysian literary prizes, as well as significant increases in philanthropists in various countries offering prizes for scientific innovations.[5] There is, in short, a widespread trend: awards, prizes, and other honors are becoming more common.

This is the process of *prize proliferation,* whereby the number of public awards grows. Observers have been commenting on this trend for several decades. In 1978, the sociologist William J. Goode noted "the contemporary proliferation of prizes and awards in almost all kinds of activities." (The number of mystery prizes had risen from five in 1946 to twenty-four in 1978.) A book published in 2005 speaks of "the unrelenting proliferation of prizes across all the many fields of culture" (that year, there were ninety-eight mystery prizes).[6]

Prize proliferation occurs throughout our society: government agencies, private businesses, schools, and other organizations all seem to be presenting growing numbers of awards; these prizes may honor either the group's own members or outsiders, and they recognize all manner of accomplishments by all sorts of people. It is impossible to calculate the total number of prizes given, let alone measure year-to-year fluctuations in that overall total. But, when we think about all of the Boy Scout merit badges, all of the student-of-the-week / employee-of-the-month designations, all of the elementary school athletic participation awards, and on and on, it is easy to estimate that there must be tens—perhaps hundreds—of millions of awards, prizes, and honors distributed in the United States each year. What accounts for this dramatic rise in public appreciation?

WHO BENEFITS?

Understanding prize proliferation requires that we take a step back and consider prize giving as a ceremonial occasion, a drama involving actors playing three roles: (1) the people giving the award; (2) the award recipients; and (3) the audience that observes the prize being given. These dramas occur all the time. At the grandest level, we have occasions like the Academy Awards ceremony, when the Academy of Motion Picture Arts and Sciences (the prize givers) awards Oscars to those who received the most votes in their categories (the prize recipients) before television viewers around the world (the audience). But there are countless, more mundane versions of these dramas, as when a Boy Scout troop holds a court of honor in a church basement, and the Scoutmaster (prize giver) distributes merit badges to the Scouts who have earned them (prize winners) before the other troop members and some of the boys' parents (audience). In order to understand prize proliferation, it helps to consider the viewpoints of each of the three types of actors in these dramas.

Award Givers

Award giving is a process involving three stages: establishment, selection, and presentation. *Establishment* includes such preliminaries as inventing the award and announcing its availability, defining the terms under which it will be awarded, providing sponsorship to cover the costs, and so on. *Selection* is the process of choosing who will receive the award, and includes identifying prospective recipients, judging their merits, and choosing those who will receive awards, as well as overseeing these activities. Finally, *presentation* involves the ceremony where the award is announced and actually given to the recipient.[7]

Prize givers seek to honor different sorts of valued qualities. Some awards designate *achievement* and are available to any eligible person who fulfills a specified set of requirements; thus the Boy Scouts' handbook spells out the requirements for becoming an Eagle Scout, and any Scout who completes those requirements will earn Scouting's highest rank. Other prizes represent *championships* and denote winning some relatively straightforward competition, so that the woman who swims the fastest 200-meter butterfly in the Olympics' final round receives the gold medal. Still other awards recognize judgments of *excellence*. These often are subject to more disagreement: the Nobel Prize for Literature is not awarded randomly (only accomplished, well-regarded writers receive the award), but it is always possible to second-guess the judges' choice and argue that someone else is more deserving. Whether prize givers view an award as denoting achievement, a championship, or excellence affects how award giving is organized.

Award giving can be more or less complex. A kindergarten soccer coach may bring a carton of inexpensive trophies to the team's last game and casually hand one to each player. At the other extreme, the process may be elaborate, drawn out, and heavily bureaucratized, with formal documents defining the honors, eligibility, and the details of selection and presentation. Awarding the Nobel Prizes, for example, is an intricate business: (1) committees for each of the six prizes are appointed by institutions (e.g., the Swedish Academy appoints the literature committee; the Royal Swedish Academy of Sciences the committees for chemistry, economics, and physics; etc.); (2) requests for nominations from which each committee, deliberating in secret, makes a choice; (3) review of the choices by the larger institutions (some committee choices are rejected at this stage); (4) notifications of the winners and the media; and (5) a week-long festival during which the awards are presented by the king of Sweden at a ritualized ceremony—the entire process overseen by the Nobel Foundation. Other award ceremonies are characterized by uncertainty about who will receive the awards, intense media speculation about the outcome, and dramatic staging before large audiences—"May I have the envelope, please?"[8]

The processes of award giving often come in for criticism. There are complaints about establishment (e.g., award categories ignore some meritorious activities, the prize itself is insufficient or inappropriate), selection (e.g., the judging is capricious, ill-informed, unfair, etc.), and presentation (e.g., the ceremonies are pompous, boring, undignified, ill-timed, etc.). Often, critics call for reform—for new or different awards, better mechanisms of selection, or more suitable forms of presentation. These complaints are not necessarily consistent; calls for a shorter Oscar telecast seem inconsistent with other proposals, such as a *Washington Post* reporter's complaint that Academy Awards tend to go to dramas: "C'mon, Oscar. In 2001, you rolled out a new award for feature-length animation. Why not extend the fun and the credit where it's due? Let's have a slot for Best Comedy. And Best Musical. Separate from each other. And if you're feeling magnanimous, we'll take some acting categories, too. Yes, for both genres."[9]

Why give awards? Award givers offer public rationales—that they want to recognize and reward exceptional performance, to bestow esteem on the deserving. Philanthropists may offer large cash prizes to promote the development of desired innovations; for instance: "The People for the Ethical Treatment of Animals offers a $1 million prize for the first to create test-tube poultry tissue that can be safely served for dinner." In these ways, awards can dramatize a group's values and, in the process, affirm its solidarity. In addition, awards may encourage and inspire others to do well, perhaps because they aspire to earn awards of their own, perhaps simply because the award helps remind them of their commitment to the group's values. Some awards are easily attained and designed to be widely disseminated—a novice Boy Scout can earn his Tenderfoot badge by mastering a few bits of Scout lore, and millions of boys have done so. Successive badges are more difficult to attain, but the awards still are attainable—so that boys are encouraged to remain involved in Scouting. Such accessible awards for accomplishments are intended to encourage good performance. In contrast, there is only one Nobel Prize in physics awarded per year; such rare awards exist to celebrate exceptional excellence.[10]

But award givers may have other, less openly articulated purposes. Arranging to offer an award serves to enhance the award givers' visibility, prestige, and influence. To the degree that the prize becomes known outside the award givers' group, that it is seen as significant, that people hope to become recipients, that news of the prize is widely disseminated, the award givers stand to gain prestige of their own. To take an obvious example, by endowing the Nobel Prizes, Alfred Nobel captured an enduring place for himself in the collective memory—in addition to promoting science, literature, and the cause of peace. Such lessons are not lost on other sponsors who establish awards to be given in their names.[11]

Prize competitions can also be an important source of income for award givers. Publishers of poetry—particularly university presses and independent publishing houses—conduct poetry competitions with substantial entry fees; the winner has his or her manuscript published by the press, while the other entrants' fees serve to cover the costs of both the contest and publication. As these contests have proliferated (there are now some 330 annually), the funding arrangements have led to charges of unfair practices in making poetry awards. Similarly, proposals to establish halls of fame often anticipate that they will attract tourist dollars, just as the movie industry hopes that the buzz that precedes—and follows—the Oscar ceremony will inspire consumers to see more movies.[12]

Award presentations also provide a means of bringing award givers into contact with award recipients. This can be particularly important if the recipients are already prestigious. Thus, a local service organization may maximize attendance at its annual fund-raising banquet by arranging to present an award to some nationally prominent figure (who may also charge a hefty fee for attending and agreeing to accept the award). On the other hand, money may flow in the opposite direction. Award recipients may be chosen in hopes that they will wind up making substantial donations to the charities that recognize their contributions.[13] In short, there are a number of ways in which award givers stand to benefit from their benevolence in bestowing honors.

Award Recipients

Those who receive awards clearly gain from the transaction. Most obviously, recipients acquire the badges, medals, ribbons, rings, plaques, trophies, sashes, statuettes, pins, patches, or other embodiments of the award. But these material tokens are merely symbols that some award giver has in fact chosen the recipient for the award. Wearing, say, a Super Bowl ring without having actually been awarded the ring for having been part of a team's championship effort is to misrepresent oneself, to perpetrate a fraud. It is having received the award, not having the ring, that is the source of prestige. Awards symbolize esteem; they affirm that one's performance has been appreciated by others. Self-bestowed awards have little value: when dictators award themselves the Grand Order of This or the Distinguished Medal for That, the larger world smirks.

In addition, some awards have direct monetary value; the winners receive cash, college scholarships, or other goods. This adds to the award spectacle; part of the initial excitement surrounding the Nobel Prize focused on the unprecedented size of the monetary awards. To gain attention, cultural awards increasingly require significant endowments. This is particularly true in the United Kingdom, where awards are often renamed after their sponsors. Thus, winners of the Mystery Writers of America's Edgar receive trophies (a small bust of Poe). In contrast, several of the British Crime Writers' Association Daggers carry cash awards and are named for corporate sponsors. For example, the award for best crime novel is currently named the Duncan Laurie Dagger (it is sponsored by Duncan Laurie Private Bank): "The prize consists of an ornamental dagger and £20,000."[14]

The benefits of receiving a prize extend far beyond the award presentation. A major award becomes a central fact in the recipient's biography, and even in the lives of his or her associates or descendants. Oscar-winning actors find themselves in demand for other movies and can charge higher rates for their services; in addition, the award usually boosts the film's profits, and may improve the prospects of others who worked on it. Similarly, a major book award can lead to increased sales, not only for the author's prize-winning volume, but for earlier books that may have attracted little attention when they first appeared, and some publishers acknowledge the importance of awards by factoring the number of prizes awarded to an editor's books into editors' annual performance evaluations. Book jackets describe authors' awards as evidence of the books' merit for prospective readers. Recipients—and their associates—can parlay the esteem represented by an award into all manner of future benefits. These can include further awards: often lesser prizes signal one as deserving consideration for even more prestigious awards. (Thus, American Nobel Prize winners in the sciences usually have been admitted to the National Academy of Sciences prior to receiving the Nobel.)[15]

Awards for excellence elicit various responses from those eligible for consideration. Some disapprove or announce their discomfort with the prize system. Some actors, for example, argue that Oscars and other acting honors debase the ideal of art by treating it as a competition; in noteworthy cases, they declare that they will not accept an award should it be offered to them. In other cases, we encounter gossipy revelations that people have mounted campaigns designed to get themselves, say, a Pulitzer Prize for Fiction.[16] The cultural ideal seems to fall between these two extremes: one should, on the one hand, show respect for the award and treat the honor as honorable (so as not to imply disrespect for the award givers); but one also should avoid being openly covetous, revealing too much ambition for receiving the prize. Striking the right balance can be tricky; it is not only children who must learn to be good winners as well as good losers.

Of course, some individuals actively seek honors. They nominate themselves or arrange for others to nominate them. Or, as more communities host marathons, bicycle races, and other athletic competitions, and as many of these offer multiple prizes, not just for males and females, but for competitors in different age categories, it has become possible to shop for less popular events with smaller fields of competitors. Carefully choosing to enter events where there are likely to be only a couple competitors in my age category can almost guarantee that I will receive a prize.[17]

There is the expectation that award recipients will appreciate, not just their prizes, but whatever esteem those awards represent. Yet this is not always true; some recipients dismiss the value of their awards or, worse, publicly challenge the enterprise that lies behind them. These doubts can create various sorts of scandals. A Vietnam-era naval officer recalls, "We joked and ridiculed these medals and ribbons. We called them 'gedunk medals,' and in the photographs I retain . . . only the career types were wearing the ribbons on their daily uniforms." Similarly, when anti-Vietnam demonstrations featured veterans throwing away their medals and ribbons, many commentators saw this as raising disturbing questions about that war. Such scandals are not limited to the military; some high-profile English cultural awards ceremonies have been disrupted when recipients denounced the activities of their awards' corporate sponsors.[18]

Advocates argue that recipients also derive benefits beyond the award itself. Pursuing the various badges that mark advancement through Boy Scouts is supposed to keep boys engaged in Scouting, so that they participate in healthy outdoor activities and develop leadership, self-reliance, and good character; Scout leaders see awarding badges as a means of keeping boys involved in a program that teaches valuable lessons. Similarly, some advocates insist that awards—particularly when given to the young—can enhance the recipients' self-esteem or otherwise foster good behavior. That is, knowing that others think well enough of you to give you an award encourages you to think well of yourself, so that you will work even harder in the future to maintain their regard. Just as the benefits for award givers depend in part on whether the award is exclusive or widely available, so do the imagined benefits for recipients.

Audiences

Award giving ordinarily occurs before an audience—the transaction involves more than just an award giver and an award recipient. In some cases, the audience is huge (the Nobel Prizes or the Oscars); in others, it is fairly small, with only a few people aware of and interested in the prize giving. Thus, a children's soccer team may distribute trophies to players at an end-of-the-season pizza party for players and their parents, while a small, specialized scholarly organization may announce awards at its annual meeting; in neither case is news of the prize likely to travel very far. Other award ceremonies are resolutely private, such as the practice of secretly awarding medals to spies and members of elite military units (even to the point of storing the physical medal in a secure place under the control of the agency making the award).[19] But, even when the number of those in the know is small, their existence is important—it is their esteem that the award denotes.

Audiences often include people with special connections to the award recipients: family, friends, and other associates who may bask in the recipient's reflected glory. In some cases, these others' assistance and support may have been essential to the winning effort (e.g., a NASCAR champion driver cannot win without sponsorship, a pit crew, and so on). Award recipients often take care to name and thank these "little people" during the presentation. When the award designates the winner of a competition—which often involves a formal entry process, so that several individuals announce their intent to compete for a prize—the audience may include contenders who didn't win. These non-recipients may display a wide range of reactions, from applauding the winner's accomplishments to challenging the decision (e.g., by complaining about unfair judging). Whereas supporters and rivals have direct connections to award recipients, the larger the award audience, the greater the proportion of people without such ties—people best thought of as spectators because they view award presentations as an entertaining or uplifting spectacle.

How does this larger audience of spectators benefit from award giving? The ceremony affirms and embodies the group's values and thereby serves as a reaffirmation of its worth and solidarity. The prize recipient's importance may even be downplayed, while the group from which the winner comes is exalted. For example, the Portuguese press responded to the announcement that the controversial novelist José Saramago had won the

Nobel Prize for Literature by paying "much less attention ... to the accomplishments of the man than to the importance of the prize for Portugal.... By describing the Portuguese language and Portuguese literature as the winners of the Nobel Prize the newspaper depersonalises the award, placing it in the category of collective achievements."[20] In addition, the presentation may be dramatic and entertaining. A full-blown entertainment awards ceremony, such as the Oscars or the Grammys, involves comedic and musical performances, extensive speculation about who will win, appearances by all manner of celebrity presenters, and the opportunity to see the winners outside the performing roles the audience is accustomed to witnessing and to watch them express various appreciative sentiments. The fact that some of these ceremonies attract huge audiences is testament to their dramatic appeal.

Organization and Incentives

Even this brief overview suggests that prizes reward, not just award recipients, but also award givers and audiences. And there are other interested parties who play less central roles in the prize-giving drama. For example, the multibillion-dollar awards and recognition industry (that is, the firms that produce trophies, plaques, and so on) naturally has a stake in encouraging award giving. And, of course, industries exemplified by particular prizes also seek to promote the process, so that the various people engaged in publishing—authors, publishers, bookstores, and so on—view book prizes as a way of fostering interest in books and encouraging book purchases. Very often, an award benefits, if not everyone, at least lots of people. Therefore, proposals to launch new awards can gain fairly broad support from prospective award givers, recipients, and audience members; often, there is little opposition to establishing a prize. Understanding this helps explain the process of prize proliferation.

RATIONALES FOR AWARDING MORE PRIZES

Of course, no one stands up and advocates general prize proliferation. Rather, the trend toward awarding more prizes is the result of many individual decisions, of lots of particular groups deciding that some particular new award is needed or at least desirable. This year, the MWA decides to establish a new Edgar award category; next year, some other association of writers or booksellers or mystery fans decides to institute a new award—or even to begin a prize program that will bestow awards in several categories. It's not that some central body decides that there ought to be over eighty prizes for detective fiction; rather, the total number of mystery awards grows as different groups of people decide that they ought to establish new honors. And the same process occurs in all sorts of social worlds, so that prize proliferation is the result of all of these actions—of increases in the number of awards in the mystery world, and the science fiction world, and the Marine Corps, the Army, and the Iowa State Fair, and on and on. Social trends emerge from the localized decisions of lots of individuals.

New awards require an argument justifying some additional, formal expression of esteem. The particular rationales offered may vary from prize to prize, but each new award is constructed as a solution to some claimed problem: there must be some sense that worthy people are not receiving all the recognition they deserve from the proposed prize givers. Most obviously, there are claims that accomplishments that are prize-worthy are being ignored: "the Nobel has served as a direct stimulus to prizes of every description, the observation that 'there is no Nobel Prize for [fill in the blank]' being trotted out as justification for every new big-ticket national or international prize in the arts." (There are many ways to suggest the Nobel-like qualities of awards. The announcements for the new Stockholm Prize in Criminology noted that: "The first prize will be awarded in Stockholm City Hall, in the same room as the Nobel Prize banquet.") But there are also claims that particular groups ought to begin to awarding prizes and thereby gain the status associated with prize-giving. Thus, the Prix Goncourt, a major French literary prize awarded by an all-male jury, led to the establishment of the Prix Femina, which had an all-female jury.[21]

Chapter 1 noted that contemporary society is marked by the proliferation of social worlds: established groups subdivide into new social worlds that create their own status systems. The growing number of social worlds means there are more arenas within which people can argue for new prizes. Members who take pride in their new social world begin to see the advantages of having an award system. Prizes embody the world's shared standards for achievement or excellence; they reveal what is valued—prized—within that world. Awards offer members guidance as to what is appreciated and recognized within the social world—a sort of map for those interested in gaining status within that world's hierarchy. In addition, prize giving itself becomes an activity that helps give the social world structure by distinguishing some members as judges, worthy of assessing what is prize-worthy within that world.[22]

The audience for a social world's prizes extends to those outside the social world. Any group that feels its accomplishments are insufficiently appreciated by outsiders can establish awards for excellence within the group. Prize giving serves to bring wider attention to the group, as well as the prize recipients; making awards "is an assertion that the contributions of the field are now worthy of public acclaim."[23] It also, of course, depicts the group giving the prizes as sufficiently distinguished to judge who deserves this recognition.

Sometimes new organizations are created for the sole purpose of awarding prizes to some underappreciated population. The history of college honor societies can be seen as an effort to expand recognition of worthy but excluded students, by bringing honors, first, to more campuses and, second, to more students in more disciplines. Membership in Phi Beta Kappa, the oldest honor society, was long restricted to liberal arts students at a relatively small number of elite institutions. This led to calls to establish other honor societies for students blocked from Phi Beta Kappa membership because they were studying in other fields (for instance, Tau Beta Pi for engineering students) or on other campuses (for example, the general honor society Phi Kappa Phi began at colleges without Phi Beta Kappa chapters). Over time, the number of these honor societies swelled (and Phi Beta Kappa, while remaining selective, itself established chapters on a growing number of campuses). Currently, there is an Association of College Honor Societies with about seventy member organizations, including sociology's Alpha Kappa Delta and Psi Beta for psychology students at two-year colleges; however, Phi Beta Kappa does not belong to this larger association. We can instantly understand the logic: a new honor society will want to join the ACHS because it wants to say, "We're just like all the other honor societies"; but Phi Beta Kappa wants no part of ACHS because it wants to claim, "We're different from all the other honor societies." Nor is honor-society proliferation limited to colleges; there are high school honor societies in many subjects, and 2008 saw the creation of the National Elementary Honor Society. Similarly, the establishment of halls of fame followed much the same trajectory: the creation of a national (now nearly forgotten) Hall of Fame in 1901 inspired the creation of many hundreds of specialized halls of fame, memorializing accomplishments within particular social worlds.[24]

Because awards reaffirm the values of the group that makes them, award recipients tend to resemble award givers. They usually share the same values, and often resemble each other in race, gender, and so on. Thus, one motivation for establishing a new social world is the sense that "people like them" are—and will always be—slow to acknowledge the contributions of "people like us"—however those categories are defined.[25]

When new social worlds are constructed as overt reactions to past disadvantage and exclusion, prize proliferation may be particularly likely. The Special Olympics movement, for instance, gives recognition to those with disabilities. Or ethnic and religious groups may host festivals featuring beauty contests and other honors for group members. The rise of the women's movement led groups at many colleges and universities to devise special award programs to recognize the contributions and accomplishments of women faculty and students. The gay and lesbian movement has led to the establishment of countless awards, such as the Stonewall Book Awards and the Lambda Literary Awards (for books), the Power in Pride Awards (for outstanding GLBT websites), and so on.[26]

Statistics can be used to demonstrate the need for awards to recognize accomplishments among groups receiving relatively fewer prizes. For example, feminist critics of Britain's Booker Prize (now the Man Booker Prize, Britain's annual award for an outstanding novel) noted that women authors won 38 percent of the awards between 1969 and 1991 and had 40 percent of the books shortlisted for consideration, yet accounted for 60 percent of novels written; this disparity helped justify calls to establish a separate award for the best novel written by a woman. But a sense of grievance is not essential. In an effort to encourage healthful exercise, some state governments have begun presenting citizens with patches and other awards for fishing, gardening, and other hobbies.[27]

The establishment of new social worlds is a major source for prize proliferation. Different organizations effectively compete for public attention when each offers a prize for the year's best movie or best mystery novel. However, there are other ways to increase the number of awards. For instance, an organization may decide to award its prizes more frequently—annually, for instance, instead of every other year—or it may designate co-winners or begin to distribute second- and third-place honors or to designate honorable mentions. Organizations also may create new award categories or subdivide existing categories (thus, the MWA began awarding an Edgar for the Best Juvenile book in 1961, then added an Edgar category for Best Young Adult book in 1989). Such subdivisions make it possible to cut even apparently small pies into very thin slices. For example, in recent years, there have been Derringer Awards—dedicated, remember, to short mystery fiction—for Best Flash (less than 500 words), Best Short Short, Best Mid-Length Short Story, and Best Long Short Story (6,001–15,000 words). Such narrow categories increase the range of activities that can lead to an award; even extremely brief pieces of fiction—presumably at a disadvantage if they have to compete with longer, more elaborate stories—can gain recognition when they have their own award category.

The possibility that prize-worthy candidates have been over-looked can inspire corrective measures. The 2009 decision to double the number of nominees for the Best Picture Oscar from five to ten was a response to "a debate about whether the Oscar voters had drifted too far from the moviegoing public," by increasing the chances that films that had attracted large audiences would be nominated. The realization that changes in the rules for selecting the Man Booker Prize had resulted in no award being given for a book published in 1970 led to a special, retrospective award being given—forty years later.[28]

There are also practices that ensure that many different people receive prizes. With several organizations offering their own best-mystery-novel-of-the-year awards, it is not unheard of for a particular book to receive more than one of these awards. However, once an author has received a particular award, many organizations seem to have informal rules against that individual receiving additional awards in that category (although it is not uncommon for people to win in more than one category, say, for an author to have won Edgars both for the Best Novel and the Best Short Story). This reluctance to have the same individual receive multiple prizes in the same category reveals the essentially honorific nature of these prizes. Contrast this practice with straightforward competitions where repeat championships are seen as something remarkable and especially admirable, such as the special prestige given to athletes who can win the gold medal in the same event in two or more Olympics.

Another form of prize proliferation involves gradually giving higher honors for the same accomplishments. A Dutch sociologist provides a nice case study of this process involving the Order of Orange Nassau, which are awards from the Dutch state for various sorts of distinguished accomplishments (including, for example, "twenty-five or forty years of 'faithful service' to one employer"). The order's awards come in eight ranks, from Knight Grand Cross (the highest) to a bronze Medal of Honor (the lowest). However, critics increasingly questioned whether this sort of hierarchy is appropriate in a democratic nation: "It is . . . at the bottom of the system . . . that the feelings of not being properly appreciated and of disappointment are so widespread"; as a consequence, the bronze medal has been effectively abandoned, and recipients get higher awards than those who had similar accomplishments in the past.[29]

Several of these trends are apparent in the military's use of medals. In the standard prize-proliferation pattern, the number of different medals has grown, the range of activities deemed worthy of being awarded medals has expanded, and the number of medals actually presented has increased. "Older awards once reserved for truly conspicuous deeds and achievement are now given out more freely. During the Persian Gulf War, Bronze Stars for 'heroic or meritorious achievement' in combat or general 'meritorious service' were given out wholesale to unit commanders." Also: "A host of new medals and ribbons recognize accomplishments not traditionally recognized in war-fighting organizations. In the past 25 years, the military has created ribbons for completing basic training, deploying on humanitarian missions, volunteering, taking part in non-hostile operations, and for making it through a four-year enlistment." This proliferation of honors leads to "medal creep": "As more get achievement medals, commanders feel compelled to reward top performers with the next level, medals of commendation."[30] At the same time, "wars today tend to be shorter and there are fewer opportunities for . . . episodes of battlefield gallantry," so that there are fewer medals for combat, even though the standards for making awards have been relaxed. No wonder "more than a dozen groups, and lawmakers are lobbying to award [the Congressional Medal of Honor] more frequently."[31]

There may even be efforts to correct past errors by reclassifying awards to make them more honorific. More than forty years after the end of World War II, the federal government upgraded the Distinguished Service Crosses (DSC) received by seven black and twenty-two Asian-American servicemen to Congressional Medals of Honor. (U.S. senator Daniel Inouye was among those honored.) The rationale for these upgrades was that no blacks or Japanese-Americans received the Medal of Honor during the war; instead, the DSC was treated as the highest award servicemen from these racial minorities could receive. Of course, such belated recognition further increases the number of prizes.[32]

Redefining eligibility for prizes often leads to more awards being granted. The Purple Heart, for example, is awarded to military service members wounded in action with an enemy. In practice, however, the boundaries of eligibility for this medal have expanded over time. During World War II, for instance, the criteria were changed so that those killed in action could receive posthumous Purple Hearts. At various times, indirect injuries caused by frostbite, smoke inhalation, or heat exhaustion have been defined as eligible, although some of these criteria have later been rescinded. A 1993 law added injuries from friendly fire, and "self-inflicted wounds now qualify for the Purple Heart, provided these occur in combat and do not involve gross negligence."[33]

There are, then, many routes to prize proliferation. There are readily available justifications for creating new prizes or for giving existing awards to more people. Theoretically, this process can continue until everyone wins—all the participants receive a trophy or at least a ribbon or certificate denoting participation. Of course, recipients should not make too much of such widely disseminated honors; this is the point of comic scenes in two recent movies (*About Schmidt* [2002]; *Meet the Fockers* [2004]) where outsiders are surprised on visiting the childhood homes of adult (thirty-something) males to discover displays of undistinguished ribbons—for participation or ninth-place finishes—from childhood competitions.

PROLIFERATION'S CRITICS

While there are many pressures that encourage prize proliferation, the trend has its critics. Often, their complaints invoke the language of inflation and economics. While there are no precise records, one discussion of honorary degrees suggests: "a guesstimate of 10,000 per year is probably in the ballpark," adding: "the honorary doctorate has fallen victim to academic hyperinflation." A film critic charges that doubling the number of Best Picture Oscar nominees represents "'cultural inflation': a growing number of opportunities for the less deserving to get a taste of ultimate victory, as part of a growing aversion to disappointing anyone." A Marine Corps officer notes: "Our present fitness report system, a system that can provide an objective means for personnel performance evaluation when applied in the spirit and intent on which it was founded, is considered bankrupt by many of our senior officers due to inflation of the quality markings by reporting seniors."[34]

The military in particular has come under criticism for its increasingly generous policies for awarding medals. Longstanding interservice rivalries foster charges of irresponsibility, such as claims about the Army "spewing out awards like they were popcorn," while "the Navy received heavy criticism for liberally awarding the Combat Action Ribbon to 30 ships during the Persian Gulf War . . . [although] many of the ships did not meet the requirements for the award." Such differences disadvantage those who restrict awards. If, say, the Army awards medals freely, while the Navy gives fewer medals, then soldiers will receive more of whatever esteem and other advantages (such as improved prospects for promotion) the honors bring, while sailors get less; moreover, the Army generally may gain more favorable publicity, thereby making it better able to compete for increased budget allocations. In such circumstances, rival organizations or social worlds cannot control each other's behavior, and the collective benefits of minimizing inflation seem much less immediate than the selfish advantages from making more awards. Why shouldn't our world's members garner the same benefits as those in rival organizations?[35]

Not everyone agrees. One Army general dismissed "the prejudice of some of our leaders against awarding 'too many medals'—no matter how richly deserved. They say they don't want to cheapen the award. To my mind, you can't cheapen an award except by awarding it to the wrong man." Thus, critics of prize inflation face an uphill struggle: medals and other awards are popular, and they are easy to defend. After all, if military medals are justified as recognition for soldiers' bravery, aren't those calling for fewer medals advocating ignoring some brave acts?[36]

Still, there are impediments that can slow prize proliferation. Organizations may restrict increasing the number of prizes they offer. The Nobel Foundation retained Alfred Nobel's five original award categories for sixty-eight years, only agreeing to add a sixth Nobel Prize (for economics) in 1969—the sole addition in the Nobels' first century. Establishing a new award requires work: someone must draw attention to the need for the new prize, and it is also necessary to work through the mechanics— how will the category be defined, how will winners be selected, how will the prize be presented, and so on. There are costs associated with making awards: people must invest time in making nominations, judging, and so on; there may be monetary costs as well—some awards carry cash prizes, and medals, plaques, and ribbons must be purchased—so budgeting becomes a consideration. Prize proliferation requires overcoming this inertia.[37]

Some arguments against awards inflation also inspire investigations of award-giving policies, calls for tougher standards, and even the revocation of awards deemed undeserved. During the Civil War, the Medal of Honor—intended to be the nation's highest military honor, given for extraordinary gallantry—was sometimes awarded for lesser acts:

> [A] shortage of manpower precipitated the award of the Medal of Honor to any member of the 27th Maine Regiment who would remain in the field beyond his enlistment. In addition, the medal was awarded to those soldiers who escorted the body of President Lincoln back to his grave site in Illinois. Fortunately, the sanctity of the Medal of Honor was restored during the early 1900s when a panel was formed to review all awards of the medal. The panel subsequently rescinded the award to those who did not receive the medal for heroic action.[38]

More often, inflation fighters finesse the question of whether awards have been going to the undeserving and simply call for setting quotas or clear standards that will restrict future awards as a means of maintaining the prize's value. Thus, when the U.S.

House of Representatives voted to limit the number of Congressional Gold Medals to two per year, the bill's sponsor explained: "The luster and importance and meaning of a congressional gold medal will be tarnished if we do not limit the number we award." (The number of these medals awarded had increased in each recent decade, from five during the 1950s, to twenty-two during 2000–2009; moreover, eight of those twenty-two went to multiple recipients—groups such as the Little Rock Nine and the Navajo code talkers.) Scandals can play an important role here. After revelations that nearly 90 percent of Harvard's class of 2001 graduated with honors led to embarrassing public criticism, Harvard's faculty devised a new policy—designed to hold the proportion of honors degrees to a mere 60 percent.[39]

Prize proliferation and symbolic inflation also cause confusion; it becomes harder to keep the various honors straight. Thus, Phi Beta Kappa—which views itself as the most prestigious academic honor society—has expressed concern about "membership resistance," that is, students turning down invitations to join: "National and local officers attribute it to an expansion of chapters at schools like state universities, where there are more first-generation college students, students who do not consult their parents on such matters, and students who have gone to public schools, all of whom are less likely to have heard of the society.... The popularity of [other honor societies] has made Phi Beta Kappa less special." After other honor societies began giving their members brightly colored honor cords to be worn with their graduation gowns, Phi Beta Kappa was forced to follow suit, lest students decide to forego an honor that could not be visibly displayed. In an environment where many honors are available, not only is the value of each individual prize diminished, but there may be confusion about an award's relative value.[40]

Critics warn that prize proliferation leads to symbolic inflation, so that awards lose their value, but their claims are easy to ignore. Because prizes are given in so many independent social worlds, because prizes stand to benefit the members of those worlds, and because warnings of inflation tend to come from people outside those worlds, the numbers of prizes—for writing outstanding mystery novels, for advancing the cause of world peace, and for participating in kindergarten soccer—continue to swell. And prizes are only the most obvious symptom of societal self-congratulation. The same issues arise on a day-to-day basis in many settings, most particularly in schools.

CHAPTER THREE

HONORING STUDENTS

"Lake Wobegon, where . . . all the children are above average."

Garrison Keillor, *A Prairie Home Companion*

For most children, starting school marks the first time they will be evaluated outside the home. Infancy and early childhood tend to be spent with family or in daycare settings where people know you as an individual, care about you, and aren't especially judgmental. School, in contrast, subjects children to expectations and evaluations, evidenced by graded schoolwork and report cards. Most family members marvel at how much small children learn during their preschool years. "She's so smart!" they exclaim. And, of course, the progress is striking as little kids learn to walk, talk, and such. But school brings together lots of these children—many regarded as wonderfully bright by their families—and the school's teachers don't have the same intense emotional ties to those kids. Suddenly it becomes much easier to compare children, and parents are confronted with how teachers—representatives of the larger world—evaluate their youngsters.

School, then, is an arena where children can gain status, not as family members who are known and loved as unique individuals, but as students. Schools create and award all sorts of status—grades on schoolwork, gold stars for neatness, placement in particular reading groups, graduation ceremonies, and on and on. Those children who do well at school become recognized as good students, and that status can give them a leg up as their lives continue. Great things will be expected of them, and they will have more and better opportunities than those given to kids labeled as discipline problems or slow learners. Children find themselves challenged to meet the school's standards, and adults fret about how well students do. Parents worry about whether their kids are doing well in school, educators worry about whether their students are learning the material, while the society at large recognizes that schools' effectiveness in teaching the young will have consequences for the nation's well-being because democracy and prosperity require a well-educated citizenry.

In other words, many people discover that they care about how schools assign status to children. This is a high-stakes process, both for the individual children whose futures are shaped by the school's judgments of their performance and for the larger society. In a sense, news that all children are "above average" would be welcome indeed—it would validate the efforts of the children, their parents, and their teachers, and bode well for the nation's future. And of course, there is a lot of fairly positive news. The proportion of young people going on to college has grown, the proportion of high school students taking Advanced Placement (AP) courses has risen, and so on.[1] Some people find those reports heartening, yet there are skeptics who remain unconvinced. They worry that many students have a weak command of basic knowledge, that schools aren't upholding high standards and can't be counted on to reward only the deserving. Educational status, like other awards, prizes, and honors, seems to have proliferated. But is this evidence that our schools actually are doing a good job, or is that just a collective delusion? Will today's students be able to meet tomorrow's challenges, or are they failing to learn what they'll need to know to compete in a globalized world?

One reason our schools come under so much criticism is that we expect them to do so many different things. Obviously, we want students to acquire basic skills—the abilities to read, write, and calculate—and we also expect them to gain knowledge, to know something about history and science, and so on. When critics charge that too many students read below grade level, or when they worry that too many don't know basic facts, they are arguing that schools are failing to teach as well as they should. But we want even more from our schools. We view the school as the key ladder for *social mobility;* all schoolchildren—whatever their backgrounds—should be able to learn and succeed and, in the process, find a route to the American Dream. We are well aware that children come from unequal backgrounds, but we would like the schools to rectify this. When critics warn that African-American and Latino students, or students raised in poverty, do less well in school, they are arguing that schools are failing to do their part to make our society more egalitarian, more just. And we have all sorts of other expectations for schools: we want children to develop creativity, learn good citizenship, and acquire discipline. But the first two sets of concerns—that students should learn the skills and information they will need to know and that schools should create mobility opportunities for their students—are especially important in shaping how people think about the sorts of status students acquire during their school years.

These concerns form the basis for two alternative educational ideologies—belief systems that explain what schools are supposed to do and how they ought to operate. Each of these two schools of thought has its own ideas about how schools ought to award status to students—ideas that seem to conflict, yet support a common outcome: awarding more educational honors.

TWO SCHOOLS OF THOUGHT ABOUT SCHOOLS

The first concern about schools comes from people who think that education is about *mastery*. That is, they view schools primarily as places where students learn a series of ever more complicated lessons; schools teach so that students can learn and master the material being taught. Diane Ravitch, one of mastery's most visible advocates, insists that schools "cannot be successful as schools unless nearly all of their pupils gain literacy and numeracy, as well as a good understanding of history and the sciences, literature, and a foreign language."[2] In this view, education should have the consequence of increasing a society's total stock of knowledge, so that more people know more. This benefits both the students (whose increased knowledge gives them valuable skills) and the larger society (which is able to advance, thanks to the increased knowledge of its members).

There is a long history of advocates who promote this vision calling for reforms that will enhance mastery, such as laws requiring that public education be available to all children or that children remain in school through a particular age or grade, and promoting innovations designed to improve how much students learn. Other mastery-centered reforms seek to expose at least some children to more sophisticated lessons; systems for academic tracking, gifted education, or AP instruction are all designed to give more able students a more demanding curriculum, so that they are not held back by classmates struggling with lessons the better students have already mastered.

This vision of schools has inspired a long tradition of educational critics who have argued that schools aren't doing enough to encourage students to master demanding material. In 1955, the best-selling book *Why Johnny Can't Read* denounced the absence of phonics from reading instruction: "the teaching of reading never was a problem anywhere in the world until the United States switched to the present method around about 1925." Only two years later, *Sputnik* inspired a national panic over the deficiencies in American math and science education. These calls for greater mastery reappear every few years. Perhaps the best-known sound bite in the mastery-centered tradition comes from the 1983 report *A Nation at Risk:* "If an unfriendly foreign power had attempted to impose on America the mediocre educational performance that exists today, we might well have viewed it as an act of war." More recently, the federal 2001 No Child Left Behind Act—designed to address complaints that American schools were "failing"—sought to establish a national commitment to mastery by requiring standardized tests that could be used to compare how well different schools were teaching their students to master the material.[3]

A commitment to mastery requires that schools have standards, the higher the better. Grades must be earned through mastery of material, and they should be reliable evidence that those standards are being met. Only tough, demanding courses of instruction can produce students whose mastery of the material will allow them to maximize their knowledge and thereby advance the interests of society as a whole.

In contrast, there is a second, rival vision offered by people who, while they certainly don't oppose students' learning, argue that schools need to emphasize providing *opportunity*.[4] In their view, the credentials students receive for completing various levels of education are keys that unlock the gates leading to desirable positions within society. That is, education is society's most important route to advancement and upward mobility, especially for students who come from poorer families. In this view, equal access to education is essential for democracy to thrive, because it is the best way to bring opportunity to all. There is a long history of opportunity-centered reforms, including the campaign against racially segregated schools (because, as opportunity's advocates famously argued, separate schools were inevitably unequal) and the more recent calls for mainstreaming (that is, keeping children with disabilities in regular classrooms as much as possible to ensure they have maximum opportunities).

Those who concentrate on education's role in providing opportunities worry about evidence that privileged students do better in school than those from lower-income or ethnic minority backgrounds, because this suggests that vulnerable students continue to face blocked opportunities. Opportunity's advocates interpret racial differences in school achievement, for instance, as evidence that schools are failing to do what needs to be done to overcome racial inequities, and they worry that schooling that leads to different achievements acts, in effect, as another form of racial discrimination.[5]

As a consequence, these advocates are likely to favor educational policies that minimize constraints on opportunities, even when students are having difficulty mastering material. Perhaps the fault lies, they argue, not with the students, but with the material being taught. Perhaps schools should modify the curriculum to make it more relevant to students' lives. After all, shouldn't schools encourage—not discourage—students, by giving them the experience of success, not failure? Those who emphasize opportunity are likely to favor policies that downplay the importance of mastery, at least in the short run. They are likely to support social promotion (advancing students to the next grade, even when they have not yet mastered the material). They may seek to purge schools of any practices that foster inequality and elitism or that damage self-esteem. Thus, some advocates call for recess that involves cooperative—as opposed to competitive—play or for avoiding using red ink to identify students' errors, on the grounds that losing at playground games or receiving red marks may discourage vulnerable students and thereby limit their opportunities.[6]

Opportunity's advocates tend to be suspicious of high academic standards precisely because those students who have trouble displaying mastery are likely to become discouraged, and children who find school too challenging early on will find it more difficult to make up the lost ground later, thereby closing off all sorts of opportunities. In this view, schools ought to cut those students some slack, to encourage them to stay in school (and to do better), to give them time to catch up, until they too achieve mastery.

MASTERY, OPPORTUNITY, AND STATUS

These two visions of what schools ought to emphasize—mastery or opportunity—have very different implications for education, and particularly for how students ought to be encouraged or rewarded through the allocation of status. For mastery's advocates, students should be challenged to learn the material and congratulated when they achieve this goal. Of course, education never ends; there is always more to learn. Yet, ideally, mastery becomes its own reward, both because the knowledge one acquires becomes a resource that can be drawn upon when trying to learn even more difficult lessons (for instance, mastering the times tables will prove incredibly useful when doing ever more sophisticated arithmetic computations) and because students come to find satisfactions in mastery (that is, knowing that you have gotten control of some subject matter is in and of itself rewarding). This means that mastery's advocates favor tough grading standards, if only because students need honest feedback. Students who make errors on the weekly spelling quiz need to be told that they aren't doing as well as they could be doing; they need to be challenged to study harder so they can do better on next week's quiz. Moreover, there is often an expectation that not everyone will achieve mastery. If all of the students in a class earn perfect scores on a spelling quiz, that suggests that the material is too easy, and that next week's quiz ought to feature a list of tougher words. The mastery model doesn't *require* that some students do less well than others, but it anticipates that school will be challenging and that, in practice, some students will outshine their classmates.

Mastery's advocates, then, see grades as important feedback; you're not doing a student any favors when you praise anything less than mastery. If an A grade is supposed to reflect outstanding performance, then a teacher should not award an A for effort, or for improvement, or for anything less than outstanding work. If a school's curriculum and its expectations for its students are sufficiently challenging, then As should be rather rare, marks of genuine distinction. Making the honor roll should be a real honor because relatively few students manage to attain that level of mastery.

At the same time, a commitment to mastery implies that you ought to have a curriculum that challenges the most accomplished students; ideally, students should be able to move on to ever more difficult material. For all students to master the material—if, say, everyone receives A grades and makes the honor roll—raises suspicions that the school isn't sufficiently challenging, that it doesn't have very high standards. (Even selective schools, those that admit only excellent students—students who might be at the top of their classes in less selective schools—should, if mastery's advocates have their way, reward their best students, assigning them status as the best of the best.)

Those who emphasize the school's role in providing opportunity are suspicious of the mastery model. They worry that children enter school with different amounts of what sociologists call "cultural capital."[7] Upper-middle-class kids tend to have better-educated parents who can afford to spend more money (and often more time) on their children's upbringing. Those parents are more likely to pay attention to child-raising experts and to follow their recommendations: they read more to their children; they "expose" them to more experiences by taking them to the library and the museum and by signing them up for more soccer teams, dance lessons, and other "enrichment" (a telling word) activities. They worry about whether their children will be prepared to pass the kindergarten readiness test, and their kids tend to show up for the first day of school knowing their colors, the alphabet, and so on. Children from these homes are said to come from "advantaged" backgrounds, and the word is apt. Their background gives them real advantages when they enter school; they have already mastered some of the school's first lessons, so they are primed to experience success right from the start.

In contrast, children from poorer families have had fewer enriching experiences, and don't start school with as many advantages; they may find themselves trying to learn material that other students already knew when they started school, so that their successes at learning may be diminished by the sense that they're just catching up to the other kids. This is very troubling to those who emphasize the school's role in providing opportunity, because much of the responsibility for giving less advantaged kids a shot in life falls on the school, and the school ought to avoid discouraging them.

This means that opportunity's advocates tend to think about rewards and status allocation in school very differently than those who emphasize mastery. In their view, children—particularly those who have not benefitted from a lot of advantages at home—need to be encouraged. The emphasis ought to be on how much they are improving, rather than on how they're falling short. The school needs to become a place in their lives where they receive support and rewards. Whereas the mastery model envisions children discovering the self-satisfactions of learning, so that they come to enjoy the challenges and appreciate the accomplishment of genuine mastery, opportunity's advocates worry that children who aren't already advantaged are likely to become discouraged when they discover that some of their classmates are already ahead, so that they may begin to assume that they can't do well at school and stop trying, thereby almost guaranteeing that they won't learn. In this view, praising some students can harm others, and opportunity advocates support policies that minimize invidious distinctions:

> All Nashville schools have stopped posting honor rolls, and some are also considering a ban on hanging good work in the hallways— all at the advice of school lawyers.
>
> After a few parents complained their children might be ridiculed for not making the list, Nashville school system lawyers warned that state privacy laws forbid releasing any academic information, good or bad, without permission.[8]

Valuing opportunity means giving all children, not just a chance to succeed, but the experience of success, so that they come to see school as an arena where they can succeed and thereby gain status. In this view, children need to be praised for what they do well, and, as a general rule, the more kids get praised and the more praise they receive, the better. The message students receive ought to be that you *can* do it, that *you* have the potential to succeed at school. This means that opportunity's advocates tend to believe that confidence-boosting rewards— status—ought to be fairly frequent and widespread. They see adopting forgiving grading standards and allowing students to move up to the next grade even when they fall short of mastery as ways of encouraging children, fostering opportunity, and—in the long run—promoting a more egalitarian, more just society.

Ideally, the ultimate outcome of all this praise and emphasis on opportunity should be mastery. Opportunity's advocates understand schooling to be a process, in which students, through encouragement, become better learners. There is nothing wrong, they would argue, with praising kids for doing less than perfect work if such praise encourages them to keep trying to do better.

Where the mastery model assumes that high grades should be relatively rare indications of true achievement, the opportunity model suggests that high grades ought to be relatively common, as a means of encouraging students to stick with, and become more engaged in, school.[9]

Mastery's advocates tend to be critical of the opportunity model precisely because it views mastery of subject matter as only one goal among several; they warn that schools should not "be expected to solve all of society's problems."[10] They may concede that praise and other positive reinforcements can guide students toward mastery, but they suspect that the opportunity model often leads to diluted standards rather than true mastery. These critics worry that the opportunity model invites relativism, in that it argues that disadvantaged kids ought to be praised for accomplishments that reflect improvement or perhaps only effort, even when those accomplishments aren't very impressive on some absolute scale. That is, schools wind up praising some kids for work that isn't all that good, which threatens to give those students a distorted sense that they're doing well enough, so that they don't see the need to attain true mastery.

Moreover, from the mastery advocates' perspective, pressures toward equity and fair treatment have another pernicious effect: once we consider some lesser accomplishment praiseworthy for less advantaged children, we may feel obliged to—simple fairness requires that we—reward more advantaged kids for the same, inferior level of performance. As a consequence, mastery's advocates charge, the opportunity model weakens educational standards. This is the road to grade inflation, to schools abandoning their commitment to mastery.

In recent years, advocates of both models have united over a concern with "our failing schools," although they've tended to diagnose the problem in different ways. Mastery's advocates argue that, if contemporary schools are failing, it is because they aren't committed to mastery and they don't hold students to sufficiently high standards. When schools promote students to the next grade before they've mastered the material, the end result is students who receive high school diplomas when they have neither the skills (e.g., at reading or math) nor the knowledge (e.g., basic understandings of science or history) we ought to be able to expect high school student graduates to have. The call for standardized testing is in large part an effort to judge school performance in terms of mastery.

In contrast, opportunity's champions insist that schools are failing because they aren't committed to opportunity, and they discourage the least advantaged students. They worry about those who drop out, because leaving school threatens to condemn young people to lives of permanent poverty. Because dropouts tend to come from poorer backgrounds, schools that tolerate dropping out are part of a vicious cycle that turns poor children into poor adults who will in turn raise their own impoverished children. Thus, opportunity's advocates want to find ways to keep students in school, to keep them from dropping out. And, when they do drop out, the advocates favor GED programs and other methods of encouraging people to return to school, to get the educational credentials they need to gain comfortable standards of living. Each camp attributes education's problems—the reasons schools are "failing"—to insufficient commitment to their own model.

This is an intense debate precisely because Americans expect our schools to do so much. We realize that our society has a lot of inequality, that some folks have a lot more money and live far more comfortable lives than others. At the same time, we claim that our society is open to advancement, so that everyone has a chance to get ahead through hard work. In order to believe that any child can make it to the top, we must envision school as the great equalizer, the place where kids who don't have many advantages can gain the skills they will need to compete successfully. And, if kids from poorer families do less well in school—get lower grades, drop out more often, and so on—this indicates that the school is failing to overcome society's inequities in the way that we like to imagine it can.

In practice, the goals of mastery and opportunity largely coexist within American education. Some teachers and administrators favor one position; others favor the other. Probably many come down on different sides when particular issues arise. Still, the mastery/opportunity distinction seems to underlie many educational debates. Should schools adopt social promotion or retain students in a grade until the material is mastered? Should schools hold to a traditional curriculum, or should what is taught change to make it more relevant to the students' interests? Do students benefit most when they are held to high standards or when they are praised for making an effort? Sincere people—people who want the best for children—can disagree about these questions, depending on how they view the nature of education.

STATUS CYCLES IN EDUCATION

People concerned with education, including parents, teachers, legislators, and educational critics, disagree about whether mastery or opportunity ought to be considered more important. This disagreement affects how schools allocate status to students. In particular, it fosters a *status allocation cycle*—an awkward term that we'll shorten to *status cycle*—in which schools, in the name of promoting mastery and opportunity, award students ever increasing amounts of status.

The cycle's dynamics are straightforward. Let's begin with a moment in the process when mastery's advocates argue that schools need to do more to encourage excellence and propose doing this by assigning some special status to students who have achieved some sort of mastery. (This is an arbitrary starting point; because this is a cycle, we could begin at any point in the process.) Some new status—a prize, a certificate, whatever—will identify those students who achieve some sort of mastery; this new distinction will serve to identify excellence. There may be considerable hoopla as the new status is unveiled, with talk about the school's commitment to excellence.[11]

The second stage in the cycle occurs when opportunity's advocates worry that awarding the new status has troubling implications. By singling out a few students, the new status leaves out many others. At least some of those who go unrecognized may feel discouraged, which could lead to devastating consequences for their schooling. Moreover, there is a good chance that those who gain the new status, on average, come from more advantaged backgrounds than those left out. In other words, the new status threatens to interfere with maximizing student opportunities. This concern leads opportunity advocates to call for reform: perhaps the number of students who receive the new status can be increased; perhaps the standards used to decide who deserves the new status can be loosened; or perhaps it makes more sense to create additional forms of recognition for at least some of the students who do not qualify for the new status. All of these reforms, of course, lead to more status being allocated to more students in the name of opportunity.

This returns us to the point where we started observing the

status cycle. The reforms promoted by opportunity's advocates leave mastery's advocates concerned that the school isn't doing enough to reward those students who achieve mastery, and they propose . . . another new status to rectify the problem. The result is a pattern of escalation. Just as prizes proliferate in the larger society, the status cycle leads to the allocation of ever increasing amounts of status in schools. To understand this process better, we can examine some debates over particular education status cycles.

GRADE INFLATION

Grades are the most basic example of school-awarded status. Grades are widely understood to be consequential: high school grades will affect whether a student gains admission to college, which colleges will admit that student, and the sorts of financial assistance available to the student; similarly, college grades influence admission to graduate and professional schools, as well as job prospects. Precisely because grades are seen as important, they lead to a status cycle.

Grade inflation (the term was coined by the sociologist David Riesman) came to public attention in 1972 with a front-page article in the *New York Times*. The report noted evidence that average grades had been rising in U.S. colleges. Innovations such as allowing students to choose pass-fail grading in some courses may have accounted for some of the increase, but the article also noted that mastery and opportunity advocates were at work: "Some younger teachers replied that grades were outdated, punitive and irrelevant anyway, and should be handed out to encourage effort, rather than to reward achievement, or to compensate for ethnic and social disadvantages. Older professors suggested with dismay that teachers nowadays had lost their nerve and self-confidence, and scramble for approval from their students by handing out high grades, instead of insisting on strict standards of achievement." One professor was quoted: "You pass [ill-prepared minority] students because they work so hard, so what do you do with the bright students who only deserve a C, but who did better than the unprepared students? Give them a C, too? No, they end up with B's."[12]

The debate over grade inflation in higher education—now nearly forty years old—hasn't changed all that much. Opponents point to rival data sets that seem to reveal that college GPAs (grade point averages) have—or haven't—been rising. Its critics insist that grade inflation is a real problem, a threat to the value of mastery. Thus, the Harvard political scientist Harvey C. Mansfield warns: "Grade inflation compresses all grades at the top, making it difficult to discriminate the best from the very good, the very good from the good, the good from the mediocre." The educational critic Alfie Kohn counters that grade inflation is a "dangerous myth": "even where grades are higher now as compared with then, that does not constitute proof they are inflated. The burden rests with critics to demonstrate that those higher grades are undeserved"; he concludes: "The real threat to excellence isn't grade inflation at all; it's grades."[13]

Critics also argue that grade inflation has occurred in high schools. Thus, one comparison of students' self-reported grades in the national Monitoring the Future surveys of 1976 and 2006 notes: "Twice as many 2006 high school students reported earning an A average in high school (15.6%, vs. 7.7% in 1976); there was also an increase in those who reported earning an A or A-minus average (32.8% vs. 18.3% in 1976)." Some of this increase may reflect

Figure 2. Popular culture conflates high grades and high standards.
ZITS © 2010 ZITS PARTNERSHIP, KING FEATURES SYNDICATE.

the practice, widespread among high schools, of assigning extra grade points to honors and AP classes. The logic behind this practice is that high school students might be reluctant to take more demanding courses lest their GPAs suffer, so a B (in some cases even a C) in an AP class may receive as many grade points as an A in a regular class. This means that students who receive Bs and Cs can have GPAs well above 4.0; in one recent year, my university announced that "more than 500 entering freshmen have GPAs of 4.00 or above."[14] (See figure 2.) Note that while opportunity advocates may encourage awarding higher grades as a means of encouraging less advantaged students, the practice of weighting grades from advanced classes in high schools probably serves to raise the grades of students from more advantaged backgrounds (who are more likely to be encouraged to enroll in those courses).

High-stakes standardized testing programs also may foster high school grade inflation. Schools care a lot about these tests because their students' scores are used to rate the schools' performance, but students do not have the same stake in the outcome. Some schools, in an effort to get students to take the tests more seriously, have awarded higher course grades to students who do well on the tests—a practice that raises grades without requiring more or better class work.[15]

VALORIZING VALEDICTORIANS

Pressures toward grade inflation are accompanied by more middle school and high school students being honored for having received high grades. Parents receive bumper stickers designating their kids as honor students. Many newspapers print the names of the students on the local schools' honor rolls.[16] Some schools distribute certificates of academic achievement, induct students into local chapters of nearly two dozen honor societies, or award academic letters for high GPAs (with pins that can be placed on the letters to denote additional years with good grades). Of course, the capstone of this recognition comes at graduation.[17]

Traditionally, many American high schools designated the one student with the highest grades the class valedictorian and allowed that student to speak at the graduation ceremony. However, a growing number of schools now name all graduates with at least 4.0 GPAs as valedictorians, sometimes leading to fifty or more students sharing the title. In schools where honors and AP grades receive extra grade points, 4.0 averages are more common than they used to be. However, calculating grades in this fashion can have the ironic consequence of discouraging naming valedictorians: "Nationwide, the movement against class ranking and valedictorians has been strongest in the highest-achieving high schools, where grade competition is so intense that students with 4.0 averages find they are far from the top of their class and do not want colleges to know that."[18]

We might imagine that mastery advocates are likely to favor

having one valedictorian, opportunity advocates more. In addition, there have been several news reports in recent years of students and their parents challenging—and sometimes filing lawsuits over—valedictorian designations. The issues can be complex. If a disabled student who was excused from PE classes is named valedictorian, is this fair to other students who had straight-A grades, except in PE? If a school considers regular attendance necessary to be named valedictorian, is it fair to deny the honor to a student with straight As who was hospitalized for an eating disorder and missed six weeks of school? In the latter case, the school district offered to name the student "honorary" valedictorian—something of a redundancy: "With the 'honorary' title, [the student] would be allowed to give a speech at the May 27 ceremony . . . [and] have her picture on the school's 'Wall of Honor,' along with the official valedictorian, . . . whose GPA was 0.07 lower. The family is considering the district's offer."[19]

Such knotty issues are more easily resolved when schools allow multiple valedictorians—and even near valedictorians. One high school principal "instituted a Row of Honor at the school's graduation ceremony for all students with a 4.0 or above GPA and a Row of Distinction for those with averages of 3.8 or 3.9."[20] In a litigious society, the ideology of mastery poses more risks for those awarding honors than does the ideology of opportunity. Overall, the number of valedictorians is likely to continue rising as schools seek to avoid disputes; instead of adjudicating among competing claims about who deserves to be the lone valedictorian, it is easier to simply award the honor to multiple students.

Similarly, there are more honors available for college graduates. At my university, a graduate may earn academic honors (summa cum laude, etc.—reflecting very high GPAs), as well as an honors degree (for taking a number of honors courses), a degree with distinction (for writing an undergraduate thesis), or an honors degree with distinction (honors courses plus a thesis). In addition, graduates may have been inducted into a variety of honorary societies, both campuswide and those associated with their particular majors. Various educational honors have become visible during the commencement ceremony. Ten years ago, graduates wore a blue cap and gown. Today, everyone receiving a bachelor's degree also has a white hood, and many graduates wear honor cords or they have one or more sashes denoting study abroad, or memberships in ROTC, sororities, and other student organizations.

DIPLOMAS WITHOUT TIERS

High school graduates designated valedictorians are at the top of their graduating classes. But what about those students who aren't contending for top honors? Some critics argue that schools have inflated grades, engaged in social promotions, and otherwise diluted their standards until the high school diploma no longer certifies the level of accomplishment that it once did. Partly in response to these critiques, many states (and some school districts within nonparticipating states) have devised systems for differentiating diplomas. These programs go by various names: advanced diplomas, honors diplomas, and so on. Such diplomas are, obviously, a mastery-centered reform. If people believe the high school diploma has been watered down to the point that it doesn't mean much, then special diplomas might be a way to identify those graduates who have met higher standards—a way of signaling prospective employers something about graduates' relative academic skills.

While there is general agreement that a high school diploma ought to mean something, proposals to award different types of diplomas often encounter resistance. In 2000, my state of Delaware announced with some fanfare that it would adopt a "three-tiered" diploma system that would affirm the state's commitment to educational standards: students would be tested in tenth grade and, depending on their test scores, would be eligible to receive a basic, standard, or distinguished diploma. Basic diplomas (to be denoted by a bronze sticker on the document) would be given to students who failed the exam but otherwise completed their high school's graduation requirements; standard diplomas (silver sticker) would go to those who passed the exam; and distinguished diplomas (gold sticker) would be awarded to those who received high scores on the exam. Students who were dissatisfied with their scores would have opportunities to retake the test in order to qualify for a higher-tier diploma.[21]

The three-tiered system came under attack, especially after it was revealed that more than half the students who took the exam during the first year it was offered only qualified for basic diplomas. News stories pointed to students with high grades who hadn't passed the test. Should a score on a single test outweigh a record of good academic performance? Critics warned that higher proportions of low-income and minority students had not received passing scores and worried that the new system marked a return to segregated schools. Protesters demonstrated outside the state capitol, waving "No More Tiers" signs. In response, the legislature passed new legislation, first postponing the implementation of the tiered system, then considering various modifications (such as allowing AP or SAT scores to substitute for the state exam), then finally, in 2005, abandoning the system altogether before a single student had received one of the tiered diplomas.[22]

Delaware's experience is not unique. Of course, the details vary from state to state, even district to district. In Charlottesville, Virginia, for instance, the requirement that students pass Algebra II in order to receive an advanced diploma led to the creation of a new course—designed "to assist students who struggled in Algebra I and Geometry" and provide an alternate way to qualify for the advanced diploma. "We felt we were denying those students an advanced study diploma," explained a chair of the high school's math department. Thus, efforts to establish differentiated diplomas have proven controversial. Most of these systems require students to pass a statewide high school exit examination (HSEE). However, "the political realities are such that policymakers are hesitant to fail large percentages of students on their examinations or to withhold diplomas from a large number of would-be graduates. Consequently, states tend to lower passing thresholds—regardless of the level of academic skills being assessed—to yield politically acceptable passing rates." In fact, "most state HSEE policies are designed to assess the mastery of skills that are learned in or before the ninth grade."[23]

The dynamics are not difficult to understand. However much critics may complain that the existing diploma system does not certify mastery, it is very difficult to implement a system that, in effect, threatens to block some people from having the opportunity to receive a status—such as high school graduate—that has been widely available.[24] Critics worry that proposals to designate different tiers of diplomas will debase the value of the traditional diploma. While opportunity advocates insist that they favor educational reforms that will improve students' mastery, they worry that sudden reforms will disadvantage vulnerable students, and they oppose penalizing those students already in the system by requiring them to meet higher standards. It is easy to propose awarding more students more status—so long as this does not seem to threaten existing opportunities.

OPPORTUNITY RIGGING

Still, opportunity advocates face a problem. They envision helping those children who have the greatest need—the have-nots, if you will—kids from poorer families, whose parents themselves have less education, who have acquired less cultural capital. And no doubt, the schools can broaden some children's horizons to some extent. But, of course, schools are by no means the only purveyors of opportunity.

Upper-middle-class families are fully aware of—and generally believe in—opportunity. They tend to believe in "enrichment." They enroll their kids in kindergarten soccer teams and see to it they have music lessons; they take them to museums and national parks. They expose them to all sorts of experiences (many of which lead to the children receiving trophies and other prizes). All of this serves to give these children of privileged families more opportunities—more cultural capital—not only in the sense that they have opportunities to play soccer or visit the museum, but also because these experiences make them more confident about their place in the world and give them impressive track records, so that when college admissions officers review the applications of kids from these "have" families, they discover records dotted with prizes and other certifications that this or that child is worthy of advancement. This is what David Brooks has called "the national pastime—rigging our children's lives so they'll be turbocharged for success."[25]

The stage is set for a sort of educational arms race—a status race—characterized by ongoing escalation. There is a lot of inequality in society, and this is particularly true in the early years of life. However much we might like to imagine infants entering the world with roughly equal potential, class makes a huge difference. In general, the higher a child's social class, the more nutritious her diet, the better the medical care she receives, the more she is exposed to adults trained to instruct and guide the upbringing of young children. This is what it means when we speak of advantaged and disadvantaged children; kids from different class backgrounds start school with very different advantages. This is why people place so much emphasis on the importance of opportunity in education: schools are supposed to reduce those disadvantages. And, as we have seen, valuing opportunity leads to recommendations that schools be a nurturing, forgiving place, where gains are celebrated and there are second—and third—chances. There should be lots of encouragement, lots of praise, lots of recognition and prizes for those who learn, because this is how we envision guiding children to opportunity.

But, of course, the school can't hope to provide opportunities that eliminate the advantages of class. All through school, children from higher class backgrounds continue to be advantaged, and whatever prizes and other forms of status the schools may dole out to poorer students are likely to be less (or less valued) than those available to upper-middle-class students—who attend schools in better funded districts and benefit from the private resources their families can invest in lessons and such. When high school students with good grades receive invitations to join a for-profit national conference for promising young leaders—an honor available to those who can afford the $3,000 tuition—the kids who wind up attending are obviously going to come from more advantaged families.[26]

Of course, opportunity advocates can do their own rigging. As we have noted, many schools host elaborate graduation ceremonies to signal the completion of middle school, even kindergarten or preschool. For instance, a variety of Internet vendors offer kindergarten graduation gear—caps, gowns, and tassels, of course, but also diplomas and class rings. Some opportunity advocates argue that middle school ceremonies "inspire at-risk students to remain in high school." But no student need do without a blowout; at affluent schools one finds proms, limousines, and the like. In 2008, Barack Obama was moved to comment: "Let's not have a huge party. Let's just give them a handshake.... You're supposed to graduate from eighth grade."[27]

IS IT JUST SCHOOLS?

In short, struggles over status allocation in schools have become commonplace. They have two causes. First, people believe that students' statuses have real, important consequences. Our society uses educational credentials to channel individuals into different career pathways: having completed high school is a prerequisite for all manner of jobs, and youths who drop out discover that they are blocked from many respectable careers; high school records—the courses students choose to take and the grades they earn in those courses—shape whether they can gain admission to college (and at which institutions); and so on.[28] Statuses awarded by schools can directly affect students' life chances.

Second, debates over educational statuses are intense because there are competing ideologies, ways of thinking about schooling and its purposes. I have described these in terms of two goals—mastery and opportunity. While most people probably consider both to be legitimate goals in theory, in practice they lead to rather different views about how grades and other educational honors ought to be allocated. The result is what I have called status cycles, where both mastery advocates and opportunity advocates find themselves endorsing proposals to allocate more status to students. Everyone is in favor of honoring students, so long as the honors go to the students they believe deserve (or need) the honors. And since a very large proportion of students have advocates speaking in their behalf . . .

Most of us passed through the school system, and plenty of folks seem to feel qualified to voice their critiques of the state of education. It is tempting to imagine that schools are a unique institutional environment, that the same constant pressure to increase status—and the institution's willingness to comply— does not occur in other settings. However, there are signs that status affluence characterizes other institutions, so that they, too, exhibit status cycles.

Consider the military. At first glance, we might imagine that this is a tough, no-nonsense profession—the near opposite of schools nurturing the young. If schools are, to use Michael Barone's term, Soft America, surely the military epitomizes Hard America.[29] And yet advancement in the military is determined by regular performance reviews or efficiency reports, as they are called. At each rank, officers are rated, and some with unsatisfactory scores are winnowed out, while those with especially high scores are placed on a fast track toward advancement. High efficiency report scores translate into faster promotions and better assignments, which in turn lead to further opportunities. Having high ratings on efficiency reports is *essential* for a military officer's advancement. In practice, getting and staying on the fast track requires uniformly excellent ratings—the military equivalent of a 4.0 average. Although, in theory, efficiency ratings are designed at least in part to identify areas where an officer might work to improve, any official record of any shortcomings can damage an officer's career prospects.[30]

The result is, as one might expect, the military equivalent of grade inflation. Both the officers being rated and those doing the rating realize that perfect scores are necessary, at least for anyone hoping to climb rapidly up the military career ladder. An officer hoping to advance "must not only assess the personality of his rating officer, but adjust his activities to conform to the professional expectations of his superior"; meanwhile, those doing the rating may experience considerable pressure to give officers being rated the benefit of the doubt, if only to avoid raising doubts about the raters' own abilities to lead and inspire their subordinates. While many inside the military are reluctant to openly criticize these inflated standards, lest their own efficiency report scores suffer, the system's "chronic inflation problem" or "inflation cancer" has led to repeated efforts to overhaul the system of officer evaluation.[31]

The marked increase in the number of medals awarded in the military reflects a related tendency to mint new, higher forms of status. One Vietnam War–era analyst noted: "By the time an officer reaches a certain rank, it is expected that he should have performed well enough to have received a number of decorations and awards. For example, it would be unusual if an officer who served in Vietnam in virtually any capacity had not been decorated with at least the air medal or the bronze star." And, in the decades following, the numbers of medals awarded continued to rise, even during periods of peace.[32]

In short, the Hard America military isn't all that different from those Soft America schools. Both students and military officers operate in institutions where evaluations have consequences, and in each case we find that the institutions respond by creating status cycles in which individuals have increased opportunities to gain status. We can expect to find similar pressures toward status inflation in any institution where individuals are evaluated according to some sort of bureaucratic scheme, such as an annual performance evaluation. The proliferation of school honors is the cousin of performance review inflation, medal inflation, title inflation (positions once called assistant deans become associate deans or even deputy deans, while analysts become senior analysts), and other mechanisms for increasing status for organizations' members.[33] In short, in all sorts of social worlds, it is possible to justify rewarding achievement using rationales akin to those adopted by education's mastery advocates and to justify recognizing more people as deserving using rationales similar to those of the school's opportunity advocates.

CHAPTER FOUR

EVERYDAY HEROES

> This show is not about me. No, this program is
> dedicated to you—the heroes. And who are the
> heroes? The people who watch this show.
>
> Stephen Colbert, *The Colbert Report*

In 1968, the Canadian branch of Purina (the pet food company)
established the Purina Animal Hall of Fame program to recognize "hero animals from across the country." In its first forty
years, the program honored 109 dogs, 23 cats, and 1 horse. (In the
United States, at least fifteen state veterinary medical associations have animal hall of fame programs, although these tend to
have separate categories for hero animals, companion animals,
and professional animals, such as guide dogs.) Most of the animals recognized for heroism have performed some sort of life-
saving action, but this can take a variety of forms; for instance,
the 2006 inductees to the Purina Animal Hall of Fame included
dogs honored for "alerting his owners to a fire started in their
barn, and saving their lives"; "persistence in drawing his owner's
attention to the early signs of breast cancer"; and "determina-
tion in tracking down an armed suspect linked to drug-related
crime."[1]

While some people may be quite comfortable with the notion of animal heroes, others may be more skeptical and doubt whether animals can understand the meanings of their actions sufficiently to be considered heroic. Even if we can imagine heroism in a dog whose actions protect or save humans, cats seem awfully self-centered and less likely to act heroically. Or is that fair? The boundaries of heroism are uncertain, even when we start thinking about human heroes. People use the word in very different ways but they seem to be applying it more often, to more people, for more reasons. Some designations of heroism provoke controversy; there are disagreements about what constitutes heroism and about which people (or animals) deserve to be called heroes. Competing definitions usually coexist, with their advocates agreeing to disagree. But sometimes debates—even scandals—emerge. Examining contemporary views of heroes and heroism reveals some of the limits of status affluence. Nonetheless, heroes, like prizes and educational honors, seem to be proliferating. To understand their spread, we need to ask what counts as heroic, and why.

THEORIES OF HEROISM

The nature of heroism is a topic that has inspired a good deal of pontification, and even a cursory review of some of these works reveals that hero is a slippery concept, one that can refer to very different things.

For instance, in *The Hero: A Study in Tradition, Myth, and Drama*, Lord Raglan examined a range of myths and folktales, and identified a sort of formula biography for the heroes of these stories (his sample included the stories of Oedipus, Hercules, Moses, King Arthur, and Robin Hood). Most of these classical heroes' lives shared what Raglan called a "pattern" of twenty-two "incidents"; while not every story featured every element, there was a good deal of overlap. According to Raglan:

The pattern, then, is as follows:

1. The hero's mother is a royal virgin;
2. His father is a king, and
3. Often a near relative of his mother, but
4. The circumstances of his conception are unusual, and
5. He is also reputed to be the son of a god.
6. At birth an attempt is made, usually by his father or his maternal grandfather, to kill him, but
7. He is spirited away, and
8. Reared by foster-parents in a far country.

And so on, right through

21. His body is not buried, but nonetheless
22. He has one or more holy sepulchres.[2]

Raglan, then, defined the hero narrowly, as a label to be used sparingly, to be applied only to towering, mythic figures.

For Thomas Carlyle, the nineteenth-century historian who coined the term *hero-worship*, heroes were not mythic, but great historical figures: "In all epochs of the world's history, we shall find the Great Man to have been the indispensable saviour of his epoch;—the lightning, without which the fuel never would have burnt. The History of the World [is] ... the Biography of Great Men."[3] Carlyle's exemplary heroes were political, religious, and literary titans, including Cromwell, Luther, and Shakespeare.

We can think of Raglan and Carlyle as offering classical, literary visions of heroism. In their views, heroes are larger-than-life—and inevitably male—figures, doers of not just great deeds, but the greatest deeds. They belong to relatively small pantheons of exceptional leaders. Raglan and Carlyle, then, presented narrow definitions of what constitutes a hero. In contrast, sociologists tend to adopt broader definitions and describe heroes of less grandeur.

Orrin E. Klapp—probably the American sociologist who wrote most extensively about heroes—located heroes within American culture's larger framework of social types. By social types, he meant those popular labels we use in everyday life to classify people, terms such as *soccer mom* and *fashion victim*. The cast of available social types shifts over time; once-familiar categories, such as flapper and beatnik, have fallen out of favor, only to be replaced by new ones, such as trophy wife and metrosexual. Klapp argued that most social types belong to one of three broad, melodramatic categories—heroes, villains, and fools.[4] He subdivided each of these broad categories according to themes relevant to American culture; thus, he classified heroes as winners, splendid performers, heroes of social acceptability, independent spirits, and group servants. Further, he broke some of these categories down by key traits; thus, his heroic winners included the strong man, the top dog, the underdog (who wins by overcoming obstacles), the brain, the smart operator, and the great lover. Each of these traits in turn generated its own set of social types: "Americans also call [the brain] genius, mastermind, Einstein, pundit (sometimes professor, brain-truster, intellectual, intelligentsia, expert, specialist)."[5]

Klapp illustrated these various types through reference to public figures, but he understood that these labels could be applied to ordinary individuals who displayed a type's distinctive characteristics. For example, his discussion of group servants includes martyrs, who "make exemplary sacrifices for group causes. What they seem to symbolize above all else is loyalty. As martyrs, Americans mention Joan of Arc, Jesus, Gandhi, Lincoln. . . . The ideal is often extended beyond supreme sacrifice to people who have suffered for worthy reasons, even pacifists and conscientious objectors are martyrs to some people."[6]

Klapp argued that Americans recognized dozens of heroic social types: "choice of heroes is almost another name for freedom. It means a wide range of opportunity—not just one door open for one kind of talent, but many." That is, he recognized that people might disagree about which acts and individuals deserved to be considered heroic, so that the label might be applied in a wide range of circumstances. But, because people disagreed about what constituted a hero, many of those labeled heroes by some might fall short in others' eyes. Klapp offered other evidence for what he called the "deterioration of the hero," noting that many admired social types were not purely virtuous, but also had flaws. This led to ambivalence and even debate about the character of visible figures, such as celebrities who "do not recognize an obligation to hold up a high standard before the public." He also noted the rise of antiheroes, which he termed *corrupted heroes.*[7]

If Raglan's and Carlyle's classical conceptions of heroes seem awfully narrow, Klapp's discussion of heroic social types seems too inclusive. Basically, Klapp considers a social type heroic if, on balance, people consider it admirable. Thus, Klapp's corrupted heroes include such types as the tough guy, the smart operator, and the wolf—all figures that warrant ambivalent admiration. Nor is it necessary that people actually use the word *hero* to qualify as a hero in Klapp's analytic scheme. Klapp reminds us that lots of people are admired for lots of different reasons, and he uses the term *hero* to encompass all of them.

Another sociologist, Alan Edelstein, favors a much narrower

definition for hero. He insists that "the United States no longer has any heroes, nor has the ability to produce new ones." He concedes that Americans behave in heroic ways (think of a fire-fighter rescuing someone from a burning building): "But these heroic actions do not necessarily make them heroes. . . . These heroic actions, brave and self-sacrificing as they may be, are generally acknowledged locally, not nationally. To be a hero is to be a national hero, and to be a national hero is to have national recognition."[8]

Edelstein argues that social changes inhibit the emergence of new, national heroes: for instance, most of us now work within bureaucratic settings that restrict our opportunities to stand out as individuals; America's population has become so large and diverse that it is difficult to find general agreement about what constitutes heroism or who ought to be considered heroic; and our media increasingly direct attention to superficial celebrities, rather than people who make significant accomplishments. Although he shares Klapp's pessimism about the deterioration of the hero, Edelstein resembles Raglan and Carlyle in his understanding that the term should be restricted to grand figures on a very prominent stage.

Frank Furedi offers a third sociological take on heroism. He, too, argues that ours is not an age of heroes: "Heroes are definitely out of fashion. The virtues of the 1990s are those of caring and suffering. At the level of the individual, these virtues celebrate the respect of limits. Not taking risks is positively advocated."[9] In Furedi's view, life in a "risk society" demands that people be suspicious of risk taking, and because heroism involves taking risks, heroes are no longer admired. Although they approach the topic from different angles, Klapp, Edelstein, and Furedi all worry that heroism may be in decline.

HEROISM'S DIMENSIONS

Clearly, theorists of heroism do not define the term the same way. They all agree that heroes are admired by others, but there is little agreement beyond that. *Hero* is a concept with multiple meanings, and before we can consider how the concept is used in contemporary America, we need to try to sort out some of these.

A first issue involves what we might call *scale*. Some theorists (including Raglan, Carlyle, and Edelstein) restrict the term to those whose reputations have endured for long times and who are known across great distances. These are mythic or historical heroes (such as Hercules and George Washington), renowned for great deeds, who form a sort of heroic elite. But other analysts (such as Klapp) define heroism far more broadly, to include all sorts of individuals and traits that are admired by others, even those (such as the smart operator) understood to have significant flaws as well as virtues. Klapp's heroic social types are far less grand than Carlyle's Great Men: the deeds for which they are celebrated are less extraordinary, and their renown is less widespread; they are what Edelstein and others call local heroes.[10] This issue of scale is key to many disputes about heroism; some commentators insist that the term be restricted to a few great figures who perform great deeds, while others are more willing to see heroic qualities in a range of less celebrated activities.

But there is also disagreement about what sorts of *qualities* ought to be considered heroic. Even those who are willing to expand the definition of hero beyond some mythic or historical pantheon to include contemporary figures may not agree about what makes a hero. Those who define heroism narrowly are likely to emphasize exceptional bravery, courage, valor. In this view, the hero risks everything, is willing to sacrifice life itself. Just as mythic heroes slay dragons, risking one's life in combat is a familiar route to being designated a hero. Thus, the Congressional Medal of Honor is awarded for gallantry "above and beyond the call of duty," and the fact that awards are often made posthumously suggests the high standards by which recipients are judged.[11]

But analogous acts in peacetime can share this quality of courageous self-sacrifice. For instance, the Carnegie Hero Fund Commission, established in 1904 by Andrew Carnegie, awards medals to "heroes of civilization": "The candidate for an award must be a civilian who voluntarily risks his or her life to an extraordinary degree while saving or attempting to save the life of another person." By restricting the awards to "civilians," the commission means to exclude, not just military personnel, but police officers and firefighters "unless the rescues are clearly beyond the line of duty and members of the immediate family, except in cases of outstanding heroism where the rescuer loses his or her life or is severely injured."[12]

Courage on the battlefield or risking one's own life to save others may not involve the titanic deeds of the classical heroes, but there is widespread consensus that these are heroic forms of conduct and that people who do such things deserve to be called heroes. But the definition of heroism has expanded beyond even these limits, so that the label "heroic," like other forms of status, is now applied to a far wider range of people and activities.

LOCAL HEROES

Today, people find heroism in other sorts of exceptional actions. Many observers have noted parallels between sports and combat—both involve a struggle against an opponent and so on. Therefore, we should not be surprised that the player who drives in the go-ahead run or scores the winning touchdown may be hailed as the game's hero, just as those who gain renown as outstanding players are celebrated as sports heroes. Sports allow people to display poise and skill under great pressure, although they rarely display death-defying courage or save others' lives. References to champion athletes as heroes have a long history, although some commentators argue that the conditions of contemporary sports—the emergence of performance-enhancing drugs, the corrupting effects of media coverage, and so on—have destroyed opportunities even for athletic heroism.[13]

Are sports figures heroes? Does it make a difference whether the athlete is a professional or an amateur? (Remember that the Carnegie Hero Fund basically excludes from consideration those who are just doing their jobs.) Should off-the-field scandals disqualify an athlete from being considered a hero? Does the nature of the sport—or of the accomplishment—make a difference? Precisely because the definition of hero is unclear, people can disagree, not just about whether athletes should be considered heroes, but about all sorts of heroism. However, it seems clear that the label "hero" is being applied in a host of new ways, often in cases when not everyone would agree that the term is applicable. Consider some examples.

Activists and Altruists

In 2008, CNN began an annual *CNN Heroes* broadcast, using the slogan "Ordinary People, Extraordinary Impact." Viewers are invited to nominate heroes in several categories: "Championing Children," "Community Crusader," "Defending the Planet,"

"Everyday Superhero," "Medical Marvel," "Protecting the Powerless," and "Young Wonder (25 or under)."[14] These categories suggest that aiding the vulnerable—children, the powerless, the ill, even the environment—is a form of heroism, analogous to saving people from more immediate threats. Of course, we know that some activists (think of the civil rights workers campaigning against segregation) risk their lives, and the combination of high risk and self-sacrifice on behalf of others resembles more traditional views of heroism.

Still, relatively few contemporary American activists lay their lives on the line for their causes. If most activism involves self-sacrifice, it usually takes the form of opportunity costs; for example, activists may be heralded for spending their own money to help others or turning their backs on lucrative career prospects in order to devote themselves to good works. Moreover, those good works need not be directed toward creating dramatic social change. A book titled *Local Heroes* offers this definition: "The local hero aims to make community life stronger, tighter, happier, richer." This definition encompasses a broad range of activities; the book profiles people who range from leaders of nationally recognized social movements (Mothers Against Drunk Driving, the Guardian Angels) to the organizers of the International [which is to say Harrisville, New Hampshire] Zucchini Festival and a Los Angeles bus driver who sings to his passengers.[15]

In this vision, any acts that serve to enhance a community's quality of life deserve to be considered heroic. The website myhero.com allows people to identify heroes, and categorizes them. Some categories (earthkeepers, lifesavers) invoke the theme of activism, but other categories, such as angels ("strangers can lift our spirits or give us hope through acts of kindness"), animals ("who have saved lives and soothed spirits"), and poets ("their words inspire us"), suggest a very broad definition of heroism.[16] Nor is it necessary to play a leading role in community organizing. My local blood bank appeals for donors with the slogan "Be a Downtown Hero," while Delaware's Office of Highway Safety's "Be a HERO" campaign encourages people to serve as designated drivers. Even such modest forms of altruism as giving blood and remaining sober can be labeled heroic.

Heroic Occupations

Discussions of heroism often assume that heroes embody prized values and that their acts involve risk or self-sacrifice on behalf of others (the soldier whose bravery saves his buddies, the firefighter who rescues a child from a burning building, the activist whose commitment and vision improve the lives of the vulnerable, and so on). In recent years, and particularly in the aftermath of the September 11, 2001, terrorist attacks, the label "hero" has been applied to whole categories of occupations, such as police officers, firefighters, and members of the military, as well as construction workers and coal miners. Consider, for example, one corporation's "Here's to the Heroes" program, in which "Anheuser-Busch is honored to salute the men and women of our armed forces and their families. Throughout 2009, members of the military and as many as three direct dependents may enter any one of Anheuser-Busch's SeaWorld, Busch Gardens or Sesame Place parks with a single-day complimentary admission."[17]

Similarly, after 9/11, the toy industry began offering several lines of action figures that portrayed "everyday heroes"; for instance, Mighty World's Emergency line included "Diego the Firefighter, Wade the Patrolman, Officer Ramon from the K-9 unit and Karen the Paramedic."[18] Similarly, the heroism of "first responders" was celebrated in a line of products depicting "Winged firefighter in fire gear holding a rescued little girl! . . . Firefighter Angel with beautiful wings, firefighters are heroes!"[19]

Of course, these are occupations where people put themselves in harm's way; they are far more likely to face physical dangers than, say, those who teach sociology. Heroic acts by police officers, firefighters, and members of the military have long been recognized through medals and immortalized through the establishment of local, statewide, or even national halls of fame. Still, there seems to be a difference between honoring as heroes firefighters who have risked—or sacrificed—their lives to rescue others and casually describing all those who serve as firefighters as heroes.[20]

Disaster plays a role here. The hundreds of firefighters and other first responders who died in the World Trade Center made visible the risks that their careers entailed. Commentators argued that anyone who took on those risks deserved to be called a hero. In particular, New York's firefighters—those who had suffered the heaviest losses in the attack—were celebrated in countless media appearances and public ceremonies; they were able to use their newly elevated status, what one analyst calls *moral currency*, to press for further advantages. A similar process of valorizing a dangerous occupation occurred after a coal mine accident in 2006; news coverage of that event also used the language of heroism to describe, not just the behavior of the miners trapped in the collapse, but the everyday courage of those who entered the mines to work.[21] When events lay bare the risks of work, it has become common to speak of the workers' heroism.

And the definition of heroism can be stretched still further.

A year after 9/11, a *New York Times* report described New York governor George Pataki's re-election campaign: "In his frequent public reflections on the last year, . . . Mr. Pataki does not claim credit. . . . Rather, he tells his audience that they are heroes. Financial exchange workers are heroes for returning downtown. Parents are heroes for consoling children. State workers are heroes for keeping services running. All New Yorkers are heroes for being decent, resilient, and tolerant."[22]

Nor did such rhetoric begin with 9/11. In his first inaugural address, Ronald Reagan declared: "You can see heroes every day going in and out of factory gates. . . . You meet heroes across a counter—and they are on both sides on that counter. . . . I am addressing the heroes of whom I speak—you, the citizens of this blessed land."[23]

When Stephen Colbert calls his television audience heroes, he is not making that big a leap.

Victims and Survivors

In Australia, just as in the United States, there is a social movement for the right to die (or "requested death") that has had some success; in 1995, Australia's Northern Territory legalized physician-assisted suicide and euthanasia. An analysis of press coverage following the law's passage found that the politician and the physician who were the movement's leading activists were portrayed as heroes, "rebels of their respective professions who had broken ranks with their colleagues." Activists "constructed the terminally ill as victims in need of rescue" from painful, cruel deaths. We have already noted the ease with which activists can be deemed as heroic, and this case invokes familiar themes—courage in the face of opposition and protection of the vulnerable. But this case also involved another set of heroes: "heroic victims." These were the terminally ill individuals who were willing to request death. This, too, involved bravery—the courage to risk social disapproval, to say nothing of being brave enough to face and accept death.[24]

Recall Furedi's warning that life in a risk society leaves no place for heroes: "Today, the fear of taking risks is creating a society that celebrates victimhood rather than heroism."[25] But contemporary culture does not draw a sharp line between victims and heroes; rather, it increasingly depicts victims *as* heroes. Suffering is recognized as an opportunity to behave heroically.

If the battlefield is a classic arena for displaying heroism, the sickbed can be understood to be a modern battlefield. We invoke military metaphors to talk about disease and treatment, particularly when the subject is cancer. Cancer is spoken of as an "enemy," one that must be "fought," "battled," and sometimes "defeated"; it "invades" and "overpowers" the body's "defenses." Physicians mount "campaigns" and politicians "declare war" against cancer.[26] In this militarized terrain, it should be no surprise to discover heroes. In fact, when doctors manage to keep terminal patients alive a bit longer, they are described as having taken "heroic measures."

Of course, the term *victim* has fallen out of favor when speaking of those who have cancer; they are increasingly referred to as "survivors" (yet another word with military connotations). Even when survival is temporary and death is understood to be inevitable, there are opportunities to display heroic behavior: "The script for heroic death begins with a depiction of the dying person struggling, sometimes against the wishes of others, sometimes against the inner self, to know the truth"; and "the acceptance of one's own death elicits considerable admiration, and is aspired to by many."[27] Terminally ill people who remain poised in the face of death, confront death realistically, continue working, and seek to leave their personal relationships in good order are valorized for behaving heroically. In other cases, those who care for the dying individual may decide that the best course is to conceal the diagnosis. Such caretakers bear the emotional burden of the impending death, and they, too, may be characterized as heroes for their sacrifice on behalf of others.

Identifying Heroes

In sum, heroes are no longer viewed simply as distant figures performing great deeds. The label is now applied to all sorts of people whose behavior is admired. A few of these may receive considerable acclaim by, say, being celebrated on CNN's annual heroes broadcast. But many will be much less well known, perhaps admired only by a few family members or friends who appreciate the courage and sacrifices involved in helping others, facing death, or otherwise managing their lives. Their heroism is indeed local, even personal. Often, heroism is a focus not so much for great public acclaim as for interpersonal admiration.

This sense that many people are considered heroes by those who know them, even though they may receive little recognition, is supported by social scientific research. Consider a survey of Philadelphia residents that asked respondents: "Do you have any heroes that you model some aspect of your life around?" Note that the question assumed that heroism attracts more than simply admiration, that it serves to inspire people to emulate the admired figures. Not counting those who declared that they were the heroes of their own lives, 40 percent of the respondents named at least one hero. Most often, the respondents named local heroes ("personal acquaintances from everyday life"); these accounted for about 40 percent of those named as heroes. The second-largest category was political figures; local and political heroes made up about two-thirds of those named—far more than heroes classified as celebrities, religious figures, and so on.[28] Another study asked children, aged 8 to 11, "Who is *your* hero?" Most children named "private heroes . . . figures that were personally known to the child," although girls were more likely to name private heroes (77 percent versus 56 percent for boys).[29] When invited to identify heroes, many people in fact point to people they know personally whom they admire. When books and television programs celebrate local heroes, they echo the views of ordinary people.

THE HERO AS METAPHOR

More than the prizes and educational honors discussed in earlier chapters, heroism is an abstraction. The term *hero* has no single, agreed-upon meaning. Theories of heroism range from those that define the term narrowly and apply it to only a few great figures to those that define it so broadly as to encompass virtually anyone who is approved of for any reason. In contemporary America, this broader definition increasingly dominates; it has become common to designate as heroes altruists and activists, people working as police officers or in other occupations that involve some risk, as well as those who handle personal challenges with poise and grace. We can suspect that the term *hero* is used more often, and applied to a broader range of behaviors, than in the past. Precisely because it has no set definition, the label is easier to apply.

Heroism is best understood as a metaphor. The classical heroes—Hercules and the like—were renowned for doing great deeds that demanded great bravery. Obviously, modern life presents few opportunities to kill nine-headed hydras. When we say that someone is a hero or that some act is heroic, we are speaking metaphorically—we are saying that this person or act is hero-like. When people do things that seem brave—not just a soldier displaying courage on the battlefield, but a social activist making a commitment to social change, or a firefighter following a career that may involve considerable danger, or even an individual coping with a terminal illness—we admire them, and we may call them heroes.

This need not involve universal acclaim. One person's hero may be another's villain. What I see as brave, you may see as foolhardy or wrongheaded. People apply the hero metaphor to very different situations, they identify different qualities as heroic, and they name different people as heroes. Just as there are many social worlds that use their own standards to decide which accomplishments are prize-worthy, just as there are competing schools of thought about the relative importance of mastery and opportunity in education, there are multiple standards we might use in identifying heroes, and we can disagree about one another's assessments.

Consider a national survey conducted in 2004 that asked respondents about three figures related to the September 11, 2001, terrorist attacks and the war in Iraq: Todd Beamer was one of the passengers on United Flight 93 who were credited with trying to seize control of the plane back from the hijackers and who died when the plane crashed; Jessica Lynch was a soldier who was taken prisoner during the initial invasion of Iraq and was recovered after a few days in captivity; and George W. Bush was, of course, the president who ordered the invasion. Respondents were asked if each was a hero. On a five point scale, with 5 indicating strong agreement and 1 strong disagreement, Beamer scored 4.33 (suggesting considerable consensus that he was a hero), Lynch 3.39, and Bush 2.64 (indicating that most people did not consider his actions heroic).[30] Still, some respondents were willing to call each of the three a hero, confirming that the term does not have a single, generally agreed-upon meaning.

When we adopt heroism as a metaphor, we inevitably simplify. Heroism is an ideal; it emphasizes virtues. But, of course, real-life people are not wholly virtuous; they display both admired qualities (bravery, altruism, and so on), and others that are less admirable. Whether a particular individual is considered heroic depends upon which features are considered salient. Should we view Columbus as an intrepid visionary, willing to risk his life sailing into the unknown, whose voyages led to the establishment of the United States, or should we see his legacy as one of slavery, disease, and colonial exploitation? Columbus's reputation has its own complicated history: at different historical moments, particular groups have emphasized particular elements in the Columbus story, so that Italian-Americans emphasized his nationality to demonstrate the importance of Italians in American history, while some contemporary Native-American activists portray him as launching Europeans' assault on the peoples and environment of the Western Hemisphere.[31] Highlighting the positive elements in the story makes Columbus a hero, but accentuating the negative parts turns him into a villain.

Similarly, claims that we live in an age without heroes often argue that we know too much about our contemporaries. They have too much media exposure, so that we are aware of their flaws and faults, and these shortcomings make the metaphor of the hero seem undeserved. Because there is always information revealing that people are not wholly good, this argument goes, we can have no heroes.[32]

The problem with this argument is already apparent: the metaphor of the hero is in fact used frequently to describe all manner of people and behaviors. Nor are there restrictions on how the term is used; a particular organization such as CNN or the Carnegie Hero Fund Commission may formally pronounce some individuals to be heroes, but nothing stops others from applying the term as they see fit. To be sure, there is never unanimous agreement: no one is considered heroic by all of the people, let alone all of the time. Instead, there are many alternative ways of understanding heroism, and the title of hero is bestowed upon lots of different people for lots of different reasons. Because declarations that someone is a hero tend to be made to audiences that are likely to agree, these claims are rarely challenged. However, the rare disputes over designations of heroism reveal some of the limits of status abundance.

CHALLENGING HEROISM

In the aftermath of the September 11, 2001, terrorist attacks, Pat Tillman received considerable publicity when he left his high-paying, high-prestige job as a safety for the National Football League's Arizona Cardinals to enlist in the Army. (*Washington Times* readers voted him the most "noble" figure of 2002.)[33] He was celebrated as a hero for volunteering for military service. The news that he had been killed in combat in Afghanistan in April 2004 also attracted intense media attention. The Army quickly processed a commendation awarding him a posthumous Silver Star, and Tillman's sacrifice was often described as heroic. Only later was it revealed that Tillman had been killed by friendly—not enemy—fire.

The facts of Tillman's death raised awkward questions and recalled the furor over Private Jessica Lynch, who was taken captive during the 2003 invasion of Iraq. Initial news reports indicated that Lynch had emptied her weapon and been wounded by enemy fire when her convoy came under attack; this suggested that she was a combat hero, and members of the congressional delegation from her home state, West Virginia, called for her to receive the Congressional Medal of Honor. After Lynch was recovered (in an operation initially depicted as a dramatic rescue, although the troops encountered almost no opposition), it was revealed that she had been injured in a vehicle accident and had been unable to fire her jammed weapon.[34]

Obviously, both Tillman and Lynch joined the Army and put themselves in harm's way; as we have already seen, by some definitions, this alone makes them heroes. But both were initially celebrated by media reports that depicted them as not just facing enemy fire, but doing extraordinary, heroic feats in combat—acts that ought to qualify them for prestigious medals. (Lynch, of course, never received the Congressional Medal of Honor, but the Army defended the decision to award Tillman the Silver Star on the grounds that he deserved the medal for trying to aid the troops in the unit whose fire killed him.) After the discrepancies between the initial hype and the facts of these cases became evident, a *New York Times* editorial asked "Who Spread False Tales of Heroism?"[35]

These examples illustrate that, although heroism is an ambiguous concept that can be defined in many ways, scandals are possible. If an individual's claim to heroism is justified by describing particular actions (e.g., Lynch was wounded by enemy fire and emptied her weapon during combat) and if those descriptions can be proven to be false, the designation of hero may be challenged and even withdrawn. Note that the individual whose actions are disputed may play no part in making any of these claims: Lynch, for example, never declared (and in fact consistently denied) that she had acted heroically; claims about her heroism seem to have been promoted by a combination of military public relations officers, cheerleading media, and over-enthusiastic politicians who joined forces to create and spread her heroic tale. When the most dramatic elements in her story proved false, backpedaling was in order.

AWARDS AND SCANDALS

Any time high status is awarded for some accomplishment, there is the possibility of scandal. Depictions of an individual as a hero may be challenged, or the justification for awarding a particular prize may prove false. Some of these scandals may become public issues and even lead to the retraction of the previously bestowed honor. Thus, a book by a professional historian arguing that gun ownership was actually not widespread in early America received the 2001 Bancroft Prize (awarded annually for a distinguished book on American history), but came under attack when evidence surfaced that some of the findings reported in the book had been inaccurately recorded (and other sources apparently did not exist), and that all the errors served to support the author's thesis—a pattern that strongly suggested impropriety. In 2002, the Bancroft Prize was rescinded.[36] Similarly, there was a heavily publicized case of a 1981 Pulitzer Prize for feature writing being withdrawn following discovery that the winning story had been falsified. Historians and journalists, of course, trade upon the assumption that what they write is true; evidence that a work is falsified undercuts its claim to legitimacy. Worse, that questionable work could be singled out for a prestigious prize calls into question the value and legitimacy of the prize itself, so that those awarding the honor must either defend or reconsider their choice.

In some cases, challenges may emerge long after the questionable award was made. The *New York Times* employed Walter Duranty as a full-time Moscow correspondent from 1921 to 1934; his writings portrayed Stalin in a sympathetic light, and Duranty received a Pulitzer Prize in 1932. Critics—particularly Ukrainians angered that Duranty failed to report the famine of 1932–33—have long called for the prize to be revoked. The issue has its own lengthy history: in 1990, the *Times* acknowledged that Duranty wrote "some of the worst reporting to appear in this newspaper"; in 2003, the paper's executive editor declared that the *Times* would not object to having the award revoked. However, the Pulitzer Prize Board "concluded . . . that there was 'no clear and convincing evidence of deliberate deception' in the articles that won the prize," and decided not to revoke the award.[37]

Nor is it necessary to have an award withdrawn. In 2004, some opponents of Senator John Kerry's presidential candidacy began to challenge his war record. (Kerry had received a Silver Star, a Bronze Star, and three Purple Hearts while serving in Vietnam.) His critics charged that Kerry's wounds—particularly the injury that led to his first Purple Heart—were too minor to have deserved medals; at the Republican convention one delegate handed out "adhesive bandages marked with Purple Hearts to mock Mr. Kerry's war wounds"; they "included a message that read, 'It was just a self-inflicted scratch, but you see I got a Purple Heart for it.'"[38] The ensuing controversy led to claims and counterclaims about questionable criteria for service medals, including revelations that "an Army general . . . put himself in for a Silver Star merely for being in Iraq," and that the military police at Abu Ghraib prison had been recommended for Bronze Stars until the notorious photographs of prisoner abuse became public.[39]

But such scandals are exceptional cases; revoking an award usually requires clear-cut evidence that the standards for assessing excellence have been violated. This may be a dual failure: first, by the award recipient for failing to have followed the rules governing scholarship, journalism, or whatever activity is being awarded; and, second, by the judges for failing to properly assess the recipient's contribution. In some cases, scandals may implicate only one of the two. For instance, when the athlete who originally received the 1988 Olympic gold medal for the 100-meter race lost his medal when testing revealed that he had used banned drugs, the prize went to another athlete, but the judges were not blamed. Or, in the 2002 Winter Olympics, evidence that biased judging had determined the outcome of the pairs figure-skating competition led to two gold medals being awarded—the first to the skaters who had received the judges' (now questionable) highest rating (who were not held responsible for having been favored and who were allowed to keep their prize), and a second to the pair who many felt should have come in first (had the judging been less biased).[40]

Although outright scandals are rare, disputes over status are common. People may disagree—even vehemently—about matters of taste, but they mostly agree to disagree. Prize competitions often design judging arrangements so as to bolster confidence in the outcome. Thus, the Olympics figure-skating competition uses a panel of judges, drawn from different countries, who use a standard rating scale. While people may grumble about the decisions, it is usually difficult to challenge the outcomes. (Moreover, some grumbling is probably desirable—it adds interest in the competition and may make the prize seem more important.) But revoking prizes remains uncommon. It requires evidence of bad behavior on the part of either the winners or the judges that, if not unambiguous, is at least very difficult to explain away.

This is why scandals over claims of heroism are so rare. We have already noted that the standards for what ought to be considered heroic are vague and subject to disagreement. If we don't agree about what makes someone a hero, how can we hope to agree on what isn't heroic? Some statements may be falsifiable: the claim that Private Lynch bravely emptied her weapon at the enemy cannot be true if the weapon was never fired. But claims that Corporal Tillman was behaving courageously when he was shot are hard to dispute, regardless of whether the fatal shots came from other U.S. troops.

CELEBRATING HEROISM

Heroes are figures of optimism; they suggest that things can get better, that some individuals do embody the virtues that society celebrates. The spread of heroism is another form of status affluence. Just as we award more prizes, and just as we lavish more praise on students, we seem willing to label more and more people as heroes and more and more actions as heroic. A term once applied narrowly to characterize great deeds by either mythic or historical figures has been broadened to encompass virtually anyone who behaves well under difficult—even potentially difficult—circumstances. Activists are heroes. Coal miners are heroes. People with terminal illnesses are heroes. A word once reserved for the extraordinary is now applied to the merely admirable.

The ambiguity regarding who or what should be considered heroic distinguishes the readiness to identify heroism from prize proliferation and other signs of status affluence. With rare exceptions, once a prize has been awarded, the matter is settled. Fans may wish that a different movie had won the Best Picture Oscar, but there is no real prospect that the award will be revoked. But heroism is different. Not everyone agrees with every assessment that someone is a hero. Standards for heroism vary, and we should not be surprised to discover that people celebrated as heroes in some social circles may be the subjects of others' disapproval. While some people remember Martin Luther King Jr. as a hero, we shouldn't forget that he was a figure of scorn—a villain—to some of his opponents. Nor does the passage of time necessarily bring consensus; Columbus's reputation today is more controversial than it was a generation ago.

There is no generally agreed-upon mechanism for identifying heroes. But the fact that no one can speak for society in designating heroes only means that everyone can designate their own. Those sociologists who worry that our society has no heroes ought to look around: there are heroes everywhere. If anything, one might argue that there are too many heroes. If everyone can be a hero, does the word still have meaning? Or is this an instance of verbal status inflation?

According to the *Oxford English Dictionary*, people seem to have begun using the term *star* to refer to outstanding performers—actors, singers, and the like—in the early nineteenth century. Thus, the *OED* quotes an 1827 issue of the *Edinburgh Weekly Journal:* "what, in theatrical language, was called *stars.*" A century later, the term *star* had been debased, and people began to refer to exceptional performers as *superstars;* thus, a 1925 novel refers to "a couple of cinema super-stars."[41] But *superstar* itself has lost much of its cachet; today, a Google search for the term produces more than 40 million hits. We now have an abundance of superstars, and we will probably need to devise a new term to distinguish the most exceptional performers from the great galaxy of mere superstars.

This illustrates the inflationary potential of status affluence. It is possible to maintain tight controls on some statuses. For more than a century, there has been but one Nobel Prize awarded for physics each year (up to three collaborators can share the award, but each award designates a particular contribution). Because the Nobel is an old, well-known, and well-established honor, and because it carries a substantial cash prize, Nobel laureates have very high status. Notice that the Nobel people cannot control the proliferation of other prizes, but they do control the designation "Nobel Prize."[42]

In contrast, there are no controls on many other statuses, including that of hero. *Hero* has no precise definition. The power to designate heroes is not restricted in any way. The result is that all sorts of people are described as heroes. Many of these descriptions are local—confined to a particular social world, perhaps only to a few people who admire someone they personally know or love.

This sense that hero is a title that has lost its meaning is reflected in references to "a genuine hero," "an authentic hero," "a true hero," and the like. Such qualifiers suggest that there may be lots of "heroes" out there, but that some are more heroic than others. (Alas, we cannot follow the lead of show business and designate superheroes—the word has already been preempted and debased by popular culture.) But, of course, there's no agreement about what qualifies as true, authentic, genuine heroism, either. Recent newspapers stories have used the label "genuine [or authentic or real] American hero" to describe a host of figures, including John McCain, John Kerry, Ralph Nader, Rudolph Giuliani, Colin Powell, Pat Tillman, Jackson Pollack, Lance Armstrong, William Lloyd Garrison, Joe Louis, Willie Nelson, Howard Hughes, Ted Williams, Charles Lindbergh—and on and on. (It is worth remembering that GI Joe toys have carried the label "A Real American Hero" and that a motorcycle jumper is billed as "Doug Danger, Real American Hero.") We lack a clear way of measuring relative heroism. On the other hand, there are many efforts to precisely rank other statuses.

CHAPTER FIVE

RANKING AND RATING

Stars are relative, not absolute, and analyzing
them represents a waste of valuable time....
I am compelled to award them because of market
pressures.... I recommend just reading the
reviews and ignoring the stars.

Roger Ebert, Answer Man,
rogerebert.com, January 9, 2005

We live in a complicated world in which we face an impossible
number of choices. The local supermarket stocks tens of thousands of different items; the multiplex will be screening more
than a dozen different movies next weekend; there are more
than three thousand colleges trying to attract students. A generation ago, someone sitting down to watch television could easily
flip through the half-dozen channels available to see what was
showing; today, viewers with up-scale cable packages or satellite reception have hundreds of choices. How to choose, how to
choose?

There are various possibilities. You might pick something
at random, or you might decide to stick with what you always
choose—because you know what to expect and there won't be

any nasty surprises. Or you might try to learn something about your options, so that you can make an informed decision. Maybe you compare prices, to find the best deal. Maybe you talk to friends to find out what they recommend. Or maybe you seek advice from someone you don't know personally, someone who has rated or ranked the various choices out there.

The ratings game has been going on for a while, but—like prizes, educational honors, and heroes—it has become increasingly widespread in contemporary America. In the 1930s, the Consumers Union began publishing information comparing different categories of consumer products; the CU continues to publish *Consumer Reports* magazine.[1] But today, there are all manner of rating services. New products—new books, movies, and other forms of popular culture; new models of cars and appliances and other consumer products; and so on—receive reviews, which often include some summary score. Thus, the movie critic Roger Ebert may award a new film four stars—his highest rating. Moreover, there are Internet sites that compile such reviews and summarize the reactions of dozens of critics. For instance, RottenTomatoes.com offers "tomatometer" ratings for movies, which divide reviews into positive and negative and then calculate the percentage of positive reviews, thereby distilling all manner of critical judgments into a single number that seems to suggest just how good critics think the movie is. Nor is a movie's quality the only issue; the Motion Picture Association of America rates new films according to its estimate of their appropriateness for young viewers.[2]

And there are the efforts to rank different phenomena. Each fall, *U.S. News & World Report* publishes its college rankings—the best known among several college ranking annuals. *U.S. News* also publishes annual rankings for graduate and professional schools and for hospitals. And there are reference books ranking cities—the best places to live, those with the lowest crime rates, and so on. People are aware of these rankings and may even help publicize them; the news that a college has improved its standing in some ranking system often is prominently displayed on the institution's website.

People pay attention to ratings and rankings because they would like to make good choices, and it helps to have information to guide them. Ratings seem to give objective information, to clarify the distinctions between alternatives. If College A is ranked thirty-sixth, and College B thirty-seventh, then somebody, somewhere, somehow has concluded that College A is in some way superior to College B. Case closed. All other things being equal, the thinking goes, a student would seem better off attending College A.

At first glance, ratings and rankings resemble other aspects of our self-congratulatory culture. Just as prizes proliferate, just as schools award more educational honors, and just as we deem an ever wider range of behaviors as heroic, ratings and rankings tend to be a way of celebrating excellence. Most often, rankings accentuate the positive: search engines identify vastly more "ten best" lists than "ten worst" lists.[3] The emphasis with rankings, as with prizes, is on identifying the best. However, the increase in ratings and rankings differs in some important ways from that of other signs of status affluence. Prizes, educational honors, and designations as heroes are usually awarded to individuals. Most often, ratings and rankings apply to products or organizations.

Moreover, ratings and rankings are more likely to be consequential. To be sure, people who win prizes or receive academic honors often gain a leg up in future competitions: Oscar winners find that they begin receiving more offers to work on other movies (and that they can expect to be paid more money on those projects); most Nobel Prize winners have previously received other exclusive honors that signal that one's work is highly regarded and therefore deserves to receive careful consideration for a Nobel.[4] But these advantages are side effects of being honored; the fact of having received an award is usually more visible, better publicized than the benefits that come from it. In contrast, the principal purpose of ratings and rankings is to provide people with information they can use to make more informed choices, so that the consequences that flow from the ranking become more important than the ranking itself.

This means that the stakes are higher with ratings and rankings than with other forms of status affluence. A favorable review can draw customers to a restaurant, but an unfavorable review can cause potential customers to stay away. The individuals and institutions subject to ratings and rankings understand both the benefits from good ratings and the risks caused by bad ones, so they have good reason to work to maximize the former and minimize the latter.

CULTURAL ASSUMPTIONS BEHIND RANKINGS

Ratings and rankings are reflections of several elements in contemporary culture. We have already noted that modern life offers an extraordinary array of *choices*. It is impossible to sample all of the wines, read all of the books, or visit all of the destinations the world offers. We cannot help but make choices. Moreover, our choices are often understood—by ourselves and by others—as indicators of our identities and lifestyles. People deliberately choose some options because those choices reinforce their self-conceptions. We all have to eat, but what we choose to eat—

and what we refuse to eat—may be an expression of a religious identity, a political ideology, and so on. Choosing kosher or vegetarian or organic foods says something about who we consider ourselves to be, and those choices are understood as meaningful by other people, as indicators of what sorts of people we probably are.[5]

Lifestyles and social worlds can be understood as formed in large part by these choices. Individuals choose to treat some things—some activities or opinions or values or whatever—as central to their lives, and these are often revealed through still other choices. Choices become status symbols in the broadest sense of the term. Choosing to drive an expensive car symbolizes one's income level, of course, but all sorts of cars—hybrids, SUVs, convertibles, and what have you—are symbols of lifestyles that reveal more than just one's social class. Various statuses are symbolized through the choices people make. As noted in chapter 1, Civil War reenactors can judge the authenticity of one another's uniforms and thereby identify different individuals' positions—status—within the reenacting world. Similarly, vegetarians can judge how knowledgeable and committed people are to vegetarianism by what they choose to eat. Most social worlds are characterized by distinctive lifestyles, so that people's choices communicate something about how they think of themselves and where they fit within both a particular social world and the larger society.

Every social world has its own status system, so that it is possible to have more or less *prestige* among reenactors or vegetarians. To the degree that people value and aspire to high prestige within a world, they will tailor their choices to meet that world's expectations. But even within social worlds, there is the problem of how to choose wisely, given the tremendous array of options. Ratings and rankings offer guidance. They can teach interested individuals which are the best choices—at least in the view of those creating the ratings and rankings. This is one reason that ten-best lists are more common than ten-worst lists: people are much more interested in learning which options are preferable—all of the others can be ignored. The understanding that the right choices can enhance one's status means that some people will view these assessments as guides to routes up whichever status ladders they aspire to climb.

Ratings and rankings also tap into cultural ideas about *expertise*. A complex society is filled with people who are recognized as having specialized knowledge, who know a lot more about some topic than the rest of us. People in traditional societies sought advice from elders who were considered wise because they had lived long enough to see more things and acquire more experience than younger people. But our society is complex enough—and fast changing enough—to make us doubt that age is the most reliable source of wisdom. Better we should ask an expert, someone who knows more than we do about some topic. Expertise in this sense does not necessarily require specialized training, but it does mean that someone has spent enough time studying a topic—and is up-to-date enough—to offer an informed assessment of various choices.

Further, our culture prefers that expertise be *objective,* so that the relative merits of the different choices are assessed in some evenhanded way. This means, first, that ratings and rankings should be devised by people who are disinterested, whose recommendations can be trusted. When we visit an auto dealership, we understand that the salespeople will try to convince us to buy one of their cars; they are advocates for their brand, not impartial arbiters of the full range of cars available through all dealers. Therefore, many people who plan to buy a car do their homework; they search for impartial evaluations such as those offered by *Consumer Reports*. The Consumers Union is well aware that their assessments are valued precisely because they are understood to be fair and evenhanded; it goes to great pains to assure people that they are an independent organization, in no way beholden to the people who make or sell the products they rate.[6] Precisely because we expect those making the assessments to be objective, revelations that some rating or ranking operation has been unduly influenced by someone who has received high scores are considered scandalous.

Often those devising ratings or rankings will spell out their methodology, the procedures they use to make distinctions among choices, in order to convince us that their evaluations are fair. Perhaps there is blind judging. Perhaps there is a panel of judges. Perhaps there will be a clearly defined set of criteria. People who understand the methods that produced the ratings or rankings are in a better position to assess the value of those judgments.[7]

One reason that ratings and rankings have become more common may be that *computing power* is more widely available. Suppose one wants to rank, say, American cities on the basis of their livability.[8] It has become relatively easy to identify a set of criteria for livability (e.g., comfortable temperatures, low cost of living, low crime rate, and so on), locate data for each of these variables (already available at the websites of various government and private entities), slap the data into a spreadsheet, devise a formula for weighting each variable, and—voila!—generate a ranked list of cities, ranging from most to least livable. It may be—it probably is—possible to dispute the resulting rankings, to argue that the formula gives too much weight to this factor and too little to another, but the information revolution has made it surprisingly easy to generate all manner of quantitative assessments of the available choices.

More important than the formula—at least so far as our cultural assumptions are concerned—is that ratings and rankings are often presented as *numbers*. Americans tend to fetishize numbers, to assume that figures imply accuracy, precision, and science.[9] Numbers seem to embody the objectivity that we seek from experts. If we give cities a livability score, and one city gets 287 points and another 286, that one-point difference provides the basis for ranking one above the other. But this is precisely the critics' point. To understand these rankings, it is necessary to take the formula apart, to understand the process that produces those scores of 287 and 286, and to assess whether it seems sensible. Yet that sort of thoughtful analysis takes time. Isn't it easier to just assume that whoever did the ranking used an appropriate methodology, that the rankings are accurate?

The demand for guidance in making choices, the widespread acceptance of independent ratings and rankings as a means for acquiring such guidance, our willingness to defer to the assessments of those deemed more knowledgeable, and the ease with which such ratings and rankings can be created ensure that we are surrounded by such judgments. To be sure, most of the time, most of us don't treat most rankings terribly seriously—we aren't interested in whatever is being ranked, or we feel capable of making our own assessments. But when we're facing a big decision with lots of options (for instance, picking which college to attend), people may search for lots of information, including rankings. While probably few people make their decisions solely on the basis of these rankings, many take them into account and give their judgments some weight.

CONTROL OF THE PROCESS

Because some people use ratings and rankings as the basis for their choices, those who are the objects of these assessments may feel vulnerable, at the raters' mercy. Ideally, they would like to control this process as much as possible. Control can rest in very different hands; although some ratings may come from independent judges, in other circumstances, those being rated may have considerable control over the process.

Consider the familiar Motion Picture Association of America's system for rating movies. Introduced in 1968, the system has evolved into the current categories: G, PG, PG-13, R, and NC-17.[10] The MPAA's movie ratings resemble other industry-run schemes for rating popular culture content, including current ratings for television programs, musical recordings, and video games, as well as earlier efforts to control the content of movies and comic books. In each case, ratings emerged after a popular culture industry came under criticism for distributing content that some critics felt might harm children. For instance, the comic book industry's Comics Code was instituted in 1955 after a heavily publicized U.S. Senate hearing in which comic books were blamed for juvenile delinquency, while the Recording Industry Association of America's parents' advisory label on music was a reaction to a 1985 Senate hearing in which rock music was linked to teen pregnancy, teen suicide, satanism, and other troubling behavior by adolescents.[11] Within popular culture industries, such campaigns raise the specter of some sort of government-managed censorship, which is likely to be cumbersome and unpredictable—something the industry would much prefer to avoid.

Therefore, in an effort to deflect officials' criticism, pop culture industries announce voluntary programs of self-regulation, such as the MPAA's movie-rating system. Their rhetoric downplays their fears that the government may begin to regulate their industry's content, even as it emphasizes their commitment to responsible behavior. They say, in effect: "We will assume the responsibility—and the costs—of evaluating our products. We will rate them, so that consumers are forewarned about content they may find objectionable." Self-regulation in the form of ratings allows the industry to demonstrate its stewardship of a public trust, even as it retains control over the rating process and avoids the threat of censorship from outsiders.

The MPAA's movie-rating system has been criticized over the years for having inconsistent, even incoherent standards. Particular language or images may justify a restrictive rating in one film, even as movies with seemingly similar content receive more lenient ratings. Because the program is funded by the major movie studios, we should not be surprised to learn that films coming from those studios—particularly when a major firm is financially troubled and has staked its future on a particular blockbuster—sometimes receive more lenient ratings. (Much of what we know about the operations of the MPAA's Rating Board dates from its early years, when the board appointed student interns. Two of the first students to hold these positions published kiss-and-tell accounts that documented the ability of major studios to engineer favorable rating decisions. Following those revelations, the board seems to have abandoned the internship program and generally manages to keep its deliberations secret.)[12] Complaints about the rating system come from members of the public, film critics, and people within the movie industry. Nonetheless, the MPAA—like its counterparts in other popular culture industries—retains firm control over the ratings process, which minimizes the ability of outsiders to interfere with movies' content. Producing its own ratings shifts responsibility: in issuing ratings, the industry has done its part by forewarning members of the audience about content they may find disturbing; if people choose to watch—or expose children to—a film they find offensive, the responsibility is theirs, not the moviemakers'.

At the other extreme, consider the Consumers Union, which seeks to maintain complete independence from the manufacturers whose products it rates. The CU maintains its own testing facilities. It devises its own scheme for rating products: "Famously, Consumers Union buys every product it reviews on the retail market like any other consumer. By not obtaining a free review copy directly from the manufacturer, Consumers Union avoids the suspicion that the manufacturer gave it special attention, producing a defect-free copy or a copy specially tuned to the requirements of the review."[13] And CU does not allow its ratings to be cited in advertising. In other words, the manufacturers whose products are being rated are not supposed to have any influence over the ratings.

These examples suggest a dimension of control over ratings that ranges from cases (like the MPAA's movie ratings) where control is internal, with ratings managed by people within the industry being rated, through cases (like the CU's ratings) where control is external, so that those doing the rating and those being rated are completely independent. There are gradations between these extremes. Most obviously, those being rated may try to curry favor from the theoretically independent people doing the ratings: movie critics may be flown on studio-sponsored junkets to sunny places where they can view a new film and interview the stars; or a restaurant that spots a restaurant critic among its diners may work to provide especially good food and service.

There can be considerable advantages to controlling—or even merely influencing—the rating and ranking process

THE CONSEQUENCES OF RANKING COLLEGES

When people pay attention to ratings, the consequences can be profound. Obviously, to the degree that people facing choices allow themselves to be guided by ratings, their behavior is affected. But, beyond that, those whose performance is being rated—the people who offer the products or services being judged—find themselves competing in a market where at least some portion of demand is driven by ratings. This leads those being rated to try to regain a level of control over the ratings process.

Here, it will be useful to concentrate on a particular case— the rankings of colleges and professional schools, and particularly those presented in annual issues of the magazine *U.S. News & World Report.* Next to a house, a college or advanced degree is likely to be the most expensive purchase many people make during their lives. Choosing a school is understood to be a consequential decision; in general, students who attend more prestigious institutions find it easier to get higher-paying jobs. And, while many students pick educational institutions conveniently located near where they live, lots of people expect to leave home and go somewhere else for their higher education, which means they may be open to a broader range of choices than for other decisions. Hospital rankings, for instance, probably aren't that influential, because most people, at least most of the time, wind up in nearby facilities where their doctors have privileges. Because they are especially consequential, rankings of colleges and professional schools have received a good deal of attention, from both the press and researchers, so they offer an especially useful—if somewhat extreme—example of how ratings work.

The first thing to realize is that people take these rankings seriously. Highly ranked colleges receive more applicants than less highly ranked colleges, because prospective students assume that their own prospects in life will be brighter if they attend the highest-ranked school to which they can gain admission. Lower rankings discourage all sorts of folks; in addition to receiving fewer applications from would-be students, colleges that slip in the rankings may receive fewer donations and find it harder to attract and retain faculty. This sets up a vicious cycle: bad rankings discourage people, so that prospective students are reluctant to apply, donors are more reluctant to make contributions, and faculty look for more promising jobs, all of which can lead to even worse rankings.[14]

Second, as the people at the institutions being ranked recognize that rankings can be consequential, they may make efforts directed at improving their standings.[15] At first glance, this might seem to be a good thing. If *U.S. News* ranks law schools on a basis of quality, then, in principle, a school might strive to improve its quality in order to improve its ranking. But, in practice, it's not that simple.

Setting out to raise one's own ranking requires understanding just how the rankings are produced. In the case of the *U.S. News* rankings of colleges and professional schools, for instance, rankings are produced through a quantitative process: for each type of institution, the magazine devises a formula by identifying a set of variables, each of which leads to a numeric score; the scores are weighted and then tallied. This gives each school a total score, allowing schools to be ranked, from the school that has the best score through the one that has the worst (although, in practice, *U.S. News* only publishes the rankings for the institutions at the top end of this scale and does not list—or rank—those scoring below some cutoff point). Getting a better score in next year's ranking requires that a school improve its overall score more than its rivals improve theirs.

Notice that it is not enough just to get a higher score, to do better than last year. If yours was the only school paying attention to the rankings, then simply improving your score might be enough to improve your standing. But in all likelihood, your competitors also will be working to improve their scores; thus your job is not just to score higher than last year, but to increase your score by more than the other schools increase theirs. Notice, too, that this is a zero-sum game. There are only ten schools in the list of the top ten schools; if your school manages to elbow its way onto the top-ten list, then your gain will come at the expense of some other school that has fallen out of the top ten. This means that every school has a stake in doing well; ignoring the rankings is very risky, even for those near the top of the standings—stop paying attention, and you could easily slip to a lower position.

The *U.S. News* system assumes that there is a single dimension of educational quality. But one reason the United States has so many colleges is that institutions were designed to serve different purposes—to educate students of particular ethnic or religious backgrounds or those who come from a particular region. Probably most colleges were founded with the justification that a new school was needed to fulfill some need that existing colleges weren't meeting. Over time, many of these institutions developed some educational programs that excelled, so that people came to think that students who wanted to study subject X would do well to attend college Y. All of these distinct missions and strengths vanish when schools are ranked on a single dimension of overall quality. Where once many schools might pride themselves as offering a good education, the rankings now mean that only one institution is best, and all others seem to some degree inferior.[16]

Actually, things aren't quite that bad. In 1983, *U.S. News* published its first rankings: based on a survey of college presidents, it listed only fourteen research universities and twelve liberal arts colleges. Of course, only a tiny fraction of prospective students can hope to reach that exclusive set of schools. The pressures of our self-congratulatory culture have led to the rankings' expansion, both to list many more schools and to acknowledge that they are of different types:

> There is not one set of rankings, but ten: national universities and (national) liberal arts colleges, four regionally differentiated sets of master's universities, and four regional sets of comprehensive colleges.
>
> Multiple rankings mean multiple sets of "top" performers who will be happy with the results and proclaim their distinction, and who will be eligible to display the America's Best Colleges award badge . . . on their Web sites and in their promotional materials.[17]

In effect, *U.S. News* first categorizes institutions into "leagues," then publishes the standings within each league. This is, then, another example of status affluence; having multiple sets of rankings allows many more colleges to be regarded as among the best—in their particular categories.

There is nothing inevitable about this zero-sum system. It is perfectly possible to use some sort of absolute scale. *Barron's,* for instance, publishes its own college-ranking volume, which categorizes schools into six tiers (including "most competitive," "highly competitive," "very competitive," and so on—

another categorization scheme that accentuates the positive). Although its criteria for being ranked in the different tiers have not changed over the years, some critics charge that these rankings have become inflated: over a ten-year span ending in 2009, the number of "most competitive" schools rose from 54 to 82, and the number of "highly competitive" schools grew from 92 to 109.[18] Absolute scales are vulnerable to charges of status inflation, which the relative rankings of *U.S. News* circumvent.

This hardly means that *U.S. News* lacks critics. After all, the magazine says that it is identifying the "best" schools, and it claims that this is not just a matter of opinion, that it applies objective standards in producing these evaluations. But how can something as abstract as quality of education be measured, quantified, and ranked? There are millions of college students who have different goals and different needs. Can a single overall measure of quality of education possibly be relevant for all of them?

And there is another, practical problem. In order to rank hundreds of schools, it is necessary to devise measures that can be quantified—numbers that can be plugged into the formula. *U.S. News* makes slight modifications in its formula from year to year, although most of these changes are modest.[19] Selecting the formula's elements involves a reasoning process that justifies using some quantitative figure to measure quality of education. For instance, we might reason that students are more likely to receive a better education when they get more personal attention from faculty (because their questions can be answered, faculty can better recognize what each student is having trouble understanding and devote more time to giving students personalized feedback, and so on). All other things being equal, then, the fewer students per faculty member, the more personal attention each student should receive. Therefore, if we divide the number of students by the number of faculty (two numbers that might seem easy to come by), we get a student-faculty ratio, which we can incorporate into our formula as one factor measuring overall quality of education.

In recent years, the student-faculty ratio receives 1 percent of the weight in the *U.S. News* college-ranking formula. Faculty compensation (that is, pay) accounts for 7 percent. Presumably this is justified by arguing that institutions that pay more can attract better faculty and better faculty provide a better education. Perhaps—although we can see how this measure would tend to give higher scores to well-endowed (usually private) schools that charge higher tuition and are located in expensive parts of the country. Faculty salary might be related to quality of education, but it is also likely to be related to other factors, as well. And why, exactly, is faculty compensation given seven times the weight of the student-faculty ratio?

Or take another example: we might argue that, if a school's graduates are satisfied with their education, then that suggests that the school provides a high-quality education. But how can we measure alumni satisfaction? How about identifying the proportion of alumni who make contributions to the school? Can't we assume that schools with a higher percentage of alumni contributors have more satisfied alumni (and therefore provide a better education) than schools with lower percentages of contributors? Right away, we have another factor for our formula—one that *U.S. News* assigns 5 percent of the formula's weight.

Rankings often involve assembling formulas that have several such elements—student-faculty ratio, faculty compensation, proportion of alumni donors, and so on. Each factor takes the form of a numeric score, these scores are weighted and then totaled, and we have an overall, quantitative measure of educational quality.

Of course, it is always possible to dispute these ratings. Surely student-faculty ratio and faculty salaries are imperfect measures of the quality of education. And there are obvious problems with using alumni giving as an index of student satisfaction (and with assuming that student satisfaction is a good measure of educational quality). For one thing, we can suspect that alumni giving is related to how well off students are; alumni with higher incomes are more likely to feel they can afford to donate to their alma maters. But it is also likely that those better-off students came from wealthier families when they began their educations; their families could afford the higher tuition at private institutions. While federal student loan programs make it possible for students from poorer backgrounds to enter expensive schools, they are likely to graduate with a boatload of debt, which is more likely to make them think twice about donating until they have their financial affairs in order. Thus: prestigious schools attract wealthier students who, after they graduate, can afford to donate to their alma maters, and those donations in turn are treated as evidence that those schools are better, setting up a new round in another status cycle.

In sum, then, rankings of higher-education institutions are consequential. College administrators discover that low rankings discourage everyone: fewer students will apply for admission, faculty may search for jobs at "better" institutions, legislators may wonder whether it is worth throwing money at less successful schools, alumni may ask themselves whether they should bother donating, and so on. It is very important to try to improve one's ranking, because rising rankings can serve as an encouraging sign for all of those audiences. (These dynamics are beginning to operate at the global level. There are now several schemes that rank universities worldwide, and political figures have begun calling for efforts to improve the standing of their countries' institutions.)[20] So colleges naturally begin to inspect the ranking formulas, to try and figure out how they might improve their standings.

GAMING THE SYSTEM

Examining the formula used by any ranking system reveals that some elements are easier to change than others. It is expensive to do much to reduce the student-faculty ratio—cutting the number of students would reduce the flow of tuition dollars, raising faculty compensation obviously increases costs, and increasing the number of faculty would boost salary costs even further. Tampering with the numbers of students and faculty threatens to ruin an institution's budget.

However, it may be possible to gain a measure of control over the ratings process in other ways. In recent years, the *U.S. News* formula has included the proportion of classes with fewer than twenty students (on the assumption that smaller classes mean students receive more individualized attention); this accounted for 6 percent of the 2008 formula, and it is easier to manipulate than some other elements in the formula. Thus, a former administrator at one university caused a minor scandal when she gave a presentation explaining how her institution managed to boost its *U.S. News* ranking. In particular, it turned its attention to class size: "[The university] has significantly increased the proportion of classes with 20 or fewer students.... [It worked] to bump sections with between 21 and 25 students down to 18 or 19, but letting a class of 50 rise to 70. 'Two or three students here and there, what a difference it can make,' she said. 'It's manipulation around the edges.'"[21] Notice that those students who could no longer get into the now-smaller classes had to go somewhere—they still needed to be taught. So the university raised the enrollment limits on other classes to handle the excess students. (*U.S. News* does include the proportion of classes with more than fifty students in its formula, but it counts for only 2 percent.) In this case, the overall student-faculty ratio need not have changed, but the proportion of classes with under twenty students improved, helping the university improve its score in the formula.

Welcome to the wonderful world of gaming the *U.S. News* rankings, where institutions pore over the magazine's formula and look for ways they can raise their scores. New graduates of one college, for instance, were offered $5 sandwich vouchers in exchange for $1 donations to their school as a means of boosting the average alumni giving rate. Some schools encourage, or even require, faculty members to take leaves in the spring to optimize student-faculty ratios, which are calculated in the fall. Still others temporarily move admitted students with lower test scores to part-time or night programs to improve selectivity scores.[22]

Similarly, a law school dean complains that competing schools "have created these artificial probation programs where students with low scores come in and they don't have to count them as part of their LSAT [Law School Admission Test]. . . . That's the rankings. We suffer because they do that and we don't."[23] In short, schools look for ways to raise their scores. If *U.S. News* counts the proportion of alumni making donations, make prospective donors an offer they can't refuse. If the magazine calculates student-faculty ratios in the fall, discourage faculty from going on leave until spring. These changes may not have any effect on the actual quality of the education your students receive, but they may lead *U.S. News* to rank your program as now "better."

Other elements in the ranking formulas may be easier to manipulate. The *U.S. News* formula includes a reputational factor—basically a measurement of how well your institution is regarded by people at other institutions. The results of this "peer assessment" are the largest single component in the college survey—25 percent. To collect these data, the magazine sends questionnaires to people at all institutions being evaluated and invites them to rate any other institutions they think they know about on a 1–5 scale.

Consider my own experience with these ratings. When I chaired sociology departments with Ph.D. programs, I would receive questionnaires from *U.S. News* asking me to rate doctoral programs in sociology. There was an obvious problem here: I knew a lot about the quality of my own department but much less about others. Of course I knew something about the departments where I had friends working, and I knew that some departments had prominent faculty or recent graduates (people who published in journals I followed or who had written books that had received a lot of attention or who had been elected to prominent positions in professional organizations to which I belonged). But this hardly amounted to detailed knowledge on my part. The questionnaires asked me not to rate departments with which I was unfamiliar. So how many should I rate? I wound up rating a couple dozen, and those ratings helped shape the rankings the magazine published. Thus, my limited knowledge and vague impressions about departments I often had never visited were used to help construct firm numeric scores said to measure relative educational quality. (Actually, there is some evidence that the reputational scores a college receives in this year's poll are affected by the institution's ranking in previous years. This creates a cycle: the formula's most important factor—25 percent, remember—in the *U.S. News* rankings reflects . . . prior *U.S. News* rankings.)[24]

Impressions like mine are used to compile the "reputational" element in the *U.S. News* rankings, and they can be manipulated in a couple of ways. A first approach is to try to improve your institution's reputation. This can be done through a public relations campaign—sending out attractive brochures touting an institution's virtues to those people who will be filling out the questionnaires from *U.S. News*. When I was department chair, I would receive such brochures telling me about the accomplishments of faculty and graduate students in other sociology departments. I often treated these as unsolicited junk mail and tossed them into the trash, but I imagine the people who sent them were hoping that some department chairs might look them over, gain a more favorable impression of the department portrayed in their brochure, and then award a higher score to the department in the next ranking.

There is a second way to affect the reputational rankings: people who are asked to rank can give their own programs or institutions high scores and give all of their competitors lower scores. After one university successfully raised its *U.S. News* ranking, there were reports that administrators on the campus systematically gave higher rankings to their own school than to other campuses. Under pressure, the university president released his rankings, which revealed that he had assigned a rating of 4 ("strong") to his own campus, and that he had given *all* other institutions rankings of 3 ("good") or lower. He explained: "I'm a hard grader."[25] Obviously, one individual's ratings aren't likely to be decisive, but every little bit helps when institutions are struggling to improve their standings by responding to whatever formula *U.S. News* has devised.

In the case of law schools, responding to *U.S. News* has become critical, because the magazine's rankings are far more visible than other ranking schemes. (Contrast this with the situation in business schools, where not just *U.S. News,* but also *Business Week, Financial Times, Forbes,* and the *Wall Street Journal*—all well-known, well-regarded business publications—publish rankings, each of which emphasizes somewhat different criteria, so that a given school may score much better in one scheme than another.[26] This opens the possibility for more schools to claim that they are among the "top-ranked" business schools.) But the *U.S. News* rankings dominate the assessment of law schools, and efforts to respond to the magazine's formula wind up having important consequences.[27]

For years, the *U.S. News* law school formula has included the median LSAT scores of admitted students as an important part of its formula, assigned 12.5 percent of the weight. (The LSAT is the standardized test taken by prospective law school students.)[28] The reasoning is straightforward: a high average LSAT score suggests that a school is selective, that good students want to go there, and that the school takes only the best. Seems sensible—but watch what happens. If schools want to improve their scores, they need to attract more students with higher scores. One way to do this is to offer more "merit" scholarships. In the past, a larger proportion of scholarship money was allocated on the basis of need—worthy students who had limited financial resources received some help. But worrying about students' financial need is a poor use of funds for law schools trying to boost their *U.S. News* ranking. It makes far better sense to offer scholarships to applicants with excellent LSAT scores—so-called merit scholarships (meaning the applicants' scores suggest that they are likely to be strong law students). But, as we all know, standardized test scores reflect social class—those differences in cultural capital discussed in chapter 3. On average, as throughout the educational system, students with top LSAT scores are likely to come from more privileged backgrounds, to have more money. In other words, when law schools work to game the *U.S. News* rankings by increasing new students' average LSAT scores, this has real consequences: money gets diverted away from need scholarships, which help less advantaged students, in favor of merit scholarships, which discount the cost of law school for high-scoring students who may have less need for financial help.[29] In other words, schools may abandon long-term goals defined by the institution (such as providing opportunities to needy students), in order to achieve short-term boosts in quality—as defined by a magazine's formula.

REBELLION AGAINST RANKING

It is not that educators are unaware of the invidious consequences of the *U.S. News* rankings. No one likes to be at the mercy of ratings over which they have relatively little control. There have been various efforts to resist the power of *U.S. News,* and the results are instructive.

First, consider the case of Sarah Lawrence College—a well-regarded institution. In 2005, the college decided to stop requiring SAT scores from prospective students; instead, it decided to use extensive samples of the applicants' writing. This might seem reasonable: the faculty at a college decide to ignore SAT scores and select students based on a careful evaluation of their writing skills. However, standardized test scores account for 7.5 percent of the *U.S. News* formula, and this change had serious consequences for the college's *U.S. News* rankings. Sarah Lawrence's president reported:

> This principled decision has put us in jeopardy. I was recently informed by the director of data research at *U.S. News,* the person at the magazine who has a lot to say about how the rankings are computed, that absent students' SAT scores, the magazine will calculate the college's ranking by assuming an arbitrary average SAT score of one standard deviation (roughly 200 points) below the average score of our peer group. In other words, in the absence of real data, they will make up a number.[30]

Ultimately, *U.S. News* decided to bump Sarah Lawrence "to an 'unranked category' . . . the rankings purgatory for colleges that can't be classified because they didn't turn in their forms or are too small or don't have enough data."[31]

While critics within higher education call for boycotts, for colleges to refuse to cooperate with the *U.S. News* rankings, many worry that rebellion would be costly. In 2007, nineteen college presidents (eighteen of whom headed institutions ranked among the top twenty-five liberal arts colleges by *U.S. News*) signed a letter criticizing the rankings and pledging that their institutions would not refer to their rankings in promotional material.[32] Of course, this step fell well short of refusing to supply data to *U.S. News* or otherwise opting out of the rankings.

This suggests the limits of rebellion against ratings and rankings. Rankings may be based on dubious criteria. Participation in rankings may be voluntary. (Remember that no one who makes a movie is required to submit their film to the MPAA's Rating Board. It's just that many theater chains refuse to play—and many newspapers won't run ads for—unrated films, so that it is virtually impossible to arrange to have audiences see your movie without receiving a rating.) But refusal to cooperate may have costs: in particular, to the degree that people pay attention to the rankings (and there is fairly strong evidence that lots of prospective students do use *U.S. News* to help them choose colleges), opting out of rankings may have many of the same negative consequences as slipping in the rankings—fewer students, fewer donations, and so on.

An alternative to open rebellion is to launch alternative ranking schemes that create other formulas. For instance, the *Washington Monthly* launched its own annual rankings. Its editors explain: "This guide asks not what colleges can do for you, but what colleges are doing for the country. It's a guide for all Americans who are concerned about our institutions of higher learning. Are our colleges making good use of our tax dollars? Are they producing graduates who can keep our nation competitive in a changing world? Are they, in short, doing well by doing good?"[33]

To measure these qualities, the magazine devised a formula with three equally weighted elements: community service (as measured by the size of a school's ROTC programs, the percentage of alumni in the Peace Corps, and "the percentage of federal work-study grant money spent on community service projects"); research; and social mobility (based on measures of the proportion of students receiving Pell Grants, a federal program to aid low-income students).[34] This formula produces very different results than the one used by *U.S. News,* and it has attracted its own critics, who question the validity of its various elements.[35] In a sense, that's the point. Any ranking scheme is vulnerable to criticism; a different formula will almost inevitably result in different rankings.

WHEN RANKINGS MATTER

The *U.S. News* higher-education rankings represent an extreme case. *U.S. News* publishes its ratings annually. The magazine's rankings don't change much from year to year—after all, the advantages that lead to Princeton's receiving a very high ranking one year aren't likely to vanish in the next. But the magazine's annual college guides sell precisely because people assume that having the most up-to-date information is valuable. We fully anticipate that many rankings will be reported at intervals—this week's best sellers and top-grossing movies, this year's annual guides ranking colleges or the livability of cities, and so on.

People read these rankings as a form of news—a way to keep track of what's happening in society—and they use them to inform their decisions. Changes—one college improves its standing, or a restaurant loses a star in the *Michelin* guide—may affect consumers' choices: more students may decide to apply to a college that has gained a higher rank, while some customers may decide to dine elsewhere.

It is not that *U.S. News* publishes the only college rankings; there are rival rankings available. There are several annual guidebooks published for prospective students, although the *U.S. News* version is viewed as being particularly influential. Under these circumstances—when people are faced with a major decision that offers lots of choices—rankings are most likely to be compelling.

Other rating and ranking schemes carry less weight. *Newsweek,* for instance, has published lists of the top U.S. high schools (ranked by the proportion of students taking AP courses—in recent years, well over a thousand schools have been able to declare themselves among the nation's best), the top global universities, the world's most powerful people, even the top fifty influential rabbis. The American Film Institute attracts attention by releasing lists of the top 100 movies, the top 100 comedies, the top 100 love stories, and so on. These lists tend to generate press coverage; the local news may report that the local high school has been designated one of the nation's best (and, not coincidentally, mention *Newsweek* in the process). Perhaps some film buffs enjoy arguing about whether the AFI's lists are correct. But these rankings are less consequential, less likely to lead to efforts to control the ranking process.

But any ranking system is vulnerable. Critics may challenge how the rankings are compiled, or they may warn that rankings don't accurately measure relative standings, or they may criticize the uses to which people put the rankings. For instance, an annual volume that ranks U.S. cities in various crime categories has drawn considerable criticism: "Within the past year the FBI posted a 'caution against ranking' message on its UCR [Uniformed Crime Reports] website, the U.S. Conference of Mayors condemned the rankings as 'distorted and damaging to cities' reputations,' and the Executive Board of the American Society of Criminology passed a resolution characterizing the rankings as 'invalid, damaging, and irresponsible.'"[36] But critics, however well reasoned their arguments, must compete against the way rankings seem to condense information into easily understood numbers. No wonder ratings and rankings increase. By emphasizing and celebrating their versions of excellence, even the least influential ratings and rankings contribute to status abundance and self-congratulatory culture.

CHAPTER SIX

THE SIGNIFICANCE
OF CONGRATULATORY CULTURE

Clearly, we live in a time and place characterized by status affluence. Many contemporary Americans are showered with esteem
and praise. They are congratulated, even as they congratulate
others. Each year, there are more prizes awarded and honors
bestowed. Each year, our schools name more valedictorians. We
designate more people—and animals—as heroes. We use ratings and rankings to carefully identify and categorize all sorts of
merit, with an eye toward highlighting the very best. Our society doesn't just foster excellence; it celebrates and promotes it.
No wonder we're self-congratulatory—we belong to a congratulatory culture.

This flies in the face of traditional sociological theories that
assume that status, esteem, honor, and prestige are scarce com-
modities, for which there is stiff competition that results in a
few winners and lots of losers. In contrast, contemporary society
seems filled with status—and we're continually manufacturing
more. Lots of people are encouraged to think of themselves as
winners—at school, at work, and at play.

Let me be clear. I have chosen to write a book about status affluence because I think it is an important aspect of our society. But it is only a part of—certainly not the whole of—the story. I am not arguing that everyone gets to win all the time. Ours is a society with plenty of inequality; there are all sorts of structural and cultural constraints on opportunity, and people face very different sorts of obstacles. Children richly endowed with cultural capital have a much easier time than kids from less advantaged backgrounds; the advantaged have better access to status and particularly to the more exclusive, more prestigious forms of status. Nothing in this book is intended to suggest that it isn't easier for people from higher-class backgrounds to win more than their share of status competitions. Still, we speak of economic affluence—the so-called affluent society— without implying that everyone is well off.[1] Similarly, the term *status affluence* implies a society with a relative abundance of status, not some utopian world where everyone is equally honored.

But how should we think about status affluence? Is it a good— or a bad—thing for a society to award lots of status? Observers disagree. The trend toward status affluence is a product of lots of campaigns to increase the supply of status—to create new prizes, to honor more students at graduation, and so on. Presumably these advocates believe that status is beneficial and that society ought to award some more. While such advocates are likely to be narrowly focused on the specific new honor they are promoting, there are those who make a more general argument that it is desirable to increase the overall supply of status in society. But, as we have seen, there also are critics who worry that too much status is being allocated, that status inflation is a real threat. In their view, status affluence is harmful. In short, reactions range from optimists who believe that status affluence is basically desirable to pessimists who see it as fundamentally dangerous. And there is even more disagreement: within both the optimists' and pessimists' camps, people disagree about why status abundance is good or bad. In order to think about the significance of congratulatory culture, it will help to begin by reviewing some of these various positions.

THE OPTIMISTS

The least critical reaction to status affluence is *naïvité*. We can imagine people whose reaction to every award announcement is straightforward appreciation—"Oh, that's great!" When someone wins a prize, they automatically assume the winner was prize-worthy. We all engage in this sort of naive acceptance much of the time, especially when we don't really know much about the arena where the award was made. Most of us are ill qualified to second-guess the deliberations that result in the annual Nobel Prizes in physics, chemistry, medicine, and economics. We don't understand in any detail what contribution led to the Nobel being awarded or why that contribution was deemed particularly significant. We simply nod appreciatively. And we have much the same reaction when we hear that all sorts of other accomplishments have been recognized: we may not know exactly why this person deserved that recognition, but it must mean something, be important to someone.

This posture of naïvité is easiest to maintain when we focus on specific allocations of status. This scientist won the Nobel— "How wonderful!" That third grader is her classroom's "Student of the Week"—"Isn't that nice!" But this naive stance ignores the larger pattern of status affluence. It doesn't think to ask what it means that more prizes are awarded, more heroes are designated, and so on. Celebrating individual awards of status fails to acknowledge that these awards are part of a larger congratulatory culture: the naive are so busy appreciating each leafy prize that they miss noticing the forest of status abundance.

Other optimists are aware of status affluence, but they argue that it is a good thing. In the view of these *promoters,* too many people have gone too long without getting the recognition they deserve: their real contributions to society have not received the recognition and appreciation they warrant. The proliferation of prizes and other forms of status is a way of correcting past errors, of giving unsung people the recognition and praise they deserve. Our first impulse might be to associate this view with the political left, with people who emphasize the need to overcome the barriers posed by the class structure, racism, and sexism, and certainly opportunity advocates in schools often invoke liberal ideology. However, arguments that additional status can rectify past neglect actually emerge in all sorts of social worlds, among whichever groups believe their members have not received the appreciation they are due. Any group that feels underappreciated, that seeks to boost its members' morale and perhaps encourage outsiders to recognize the group's worth, is able to justify minting awards and other forms of status. Such feelings of disenchantment with the recognition one's group receives, as well as pride in the group's accomplishments, are widespread. Conservatives and fundamentalists seem no less likely to allocate status to those who share their views than liberals and feminists. Promoters, in short, favor more status for those in their social worlds although, like the naive, they tend to be more-or-less oblivious to the larger pattern of status affluence, to the way that each successful promotion contributes to increasing the overall supply of status.

In contrast, a third category of optimist—what we might call the *enthusiasts*—acknowledges that status is increasing, but argues that more status serves positive social ends, that it makes society better. In recent years these arguments often invoke the concept of self-esteem.[2] In this view, most social problems have their roots in inadequate self-esteem. Dropping out of school, teenage pregnancy, drug abuse, obesity, alcoholism, depression, suicide, and a long list of other social ills can be explained as products of low self-esteem. People make bad decisions because they don't think well of themselves.

If low self-esteem causes problems, then enhancing self-esteem offers at least a partial solution—a route toward mitigating those problems. Get people to stop beating themselves up, and they'll start making better choices. And one way to improve self-esteem is to provide more *social* esteem, by increasing the supply of status. Give people the sense that others think well of them, and they should come to think better of themselves and, as a consequence of this increased self-esteem, make better choices. Thus, giving more people prizes, awarding more students educational honors, and designating more people as heroes all become ways of enhancing self-esteem and thereby improving society.

For these enthusiasts, status affluence is therapeutic, a way of healing wounded self-esteem. This approach is especially favored by some educators, who view childhood as the key time of life and schools as an arena where self-esteem can be either built or destroyed. They argue that the experience of failure damages self-esteem, and they search for ways of teaching that minimize risks. On the playground, this involves adopting non-competitive games and activities, so that no one risks being a loser. In the classroom, children should be praised and encouraged, not criticized and discouraged.[3] Making every child feel like a winner becomes a strategy for building a better society.

For enthusiasts, then, status affluence is not just evidence that we live in a world of excellence; it is actually a strategy for making that world even better. Status affluence, like economic affluence, has the potential to improve the lives of all people it touches. For the enthusiasts, claims that either of these forms of affluence may not benefit all people equally, or that those most disadvantaged may benefit the least, should be taken as arguments not for halting the spread of affluence but rather for working to help those whose needs are greater receive the benefits of affluence. But not everyone agrees.

THE PESSIMISTS

Status affluence also has its critics, pessimists who view it as ultimately damaging to society. Their critiques take two basic approaches—one often favored by critics on the right, the other more by those on the left. However, neither of these critiques is ideologically pure, and there are some liberals and some conservatives voicing each complaint.

Status Inflation Undermines the Social Order

The first pessimistic critique—often voiced by conservatives—warns that too many prizes and other forms of abundant status discourage standards and damage character. These critics are usually the ones warning about status inflation. In their view, status serves an important function for society: status affirms the moral order; it signals what is admired and valued. By honoring its members' best achievements, society encourages desirable behavior. In this view, status inflation is a problem because awarding status for less than exceptional accomplishments and praising what is less than excellent as good enough destroys society's moral compass and encourages mediocrity. (This is a more general version of the mastery position outlined in chapter 3.)

This critique argues that individuals who experience status abundance may suffer damaged characters. These critics are suspicious of efforts to boost self-esteem through praise. Too much praise is inflationary; when praise is not rare, its value is debased. Worse, it can give those who receive the praise a distorted, inflated sense of their own worth. In sharp contrast to those enthusiasts seeking to boost self-esteem, these critics argue that children raised on a diet rich in praise have, if anything, too much self-esteem: they think too well of themselves and come to expect—to believe—that they deserve continual appreciation for their accomplishments. They become, to use an old expression, spoiled.

This argument is supported by anecdotal reports that corporations are finding younger workers become disenchanted and discouraged, not just when they are criticized, but also when they aren't praised sufficiently. Journalists write articles with titles such as: "Are We Raising a Nation of Little Egomaniacs?," "Has Generation Y Overdosed on Self-Esteem?," and "Most-Praised Generation Craves Kudos at the Office."[4] Their reports also point to social-scientific findings that seem to document trends toward young people feeling entitled to praise:

- A study of "self-entitled college students" found that 41 percent of students surveyed agreed with the statement "If I have completed most of the reading for a class, I deserve a B in that course"; 34 percent agreed that "If I have attended most classes for a course, I deserve at least a grade of B."[5]

- An analysis of adolescents' expectations suggests "that high school seniors have become progressively more unrealistic about their future achievements," that is, that there is a growing tendency for students with relatively weak high school records to assume that they will be able to obtain graduate degrees and pursue professional careers. The authors account for this trend by pointing to "institutional trends in the educational system such as grade inflation and college-for-all norms," and argue that the result is "ambition inflation" that will lead to disappointment for many.[6]

- Two psychologists—authors of a book titled *The Narcissism Epidemic*—point to a rising tide of self-approval, "with more than 80% of recent college students scoring higher in general self-esteem than the average 1960s college student." They warn:

    The lifecourse of the generation of Americans just now entering the workforce will be especially interesting to watch. Their parents and teachers gave them inflated feedback. . . . They got trophies just for showing up as kids, but as adults many of them might be struggling just to find a job. The culture of the last few decades has not prepared this generation for the challenges they will face. Many will rise to the occasion, buckling down to work harder. The rest will be angry and depressed at their lot in life, so different from the comfort they were led to expect would be theirs.[7]

Some researchers also challenge the assumptions made by some optimists that praise and status are generally beneficial. Thus, a review of the psychological literature on the effects of praise on children's motivation is decidedly guarded; the authors argue that those effects "are both complex and diverse, ranging from beneficial to negligible, to detrimental." In particular, they warn that negative effects are likely when praise is viewed as insincere, that is, when it is "overly general or "highly effusive." Moreover, "when children are praised for accomplishments that are achieved easily by others, they may view praise as an indication of their low ability."[8] Similarly, an extensive review of research on self-esteem concludes:

> Raising self-esteem will not by itself make young people perform better in school, obey the law, stay out of trouble, get along better with their fellows, or respect the rights of others, among many other desirable outcomes. However, it does seem appropriate to try to boost people's self-esteem as a reward for ethical behavior and worthy achievements. . . . By the same token, we think it appropriate and even essential to criticize harmful or unethical behavior and lazy or deficient performance, without worrying that someone's self-esteem might be reduced.[9]

These overviews of bodies of research concerning praise and self-esteem have implications for status affluence. Whereas some optimists assume that distributing more prizes and other forms of status must surely boost self-esteem and encourage the disadvantaged to achieve, the data hardly encourage confidence in these outcomes.

Thus, some pessimists warn that status affluence will lead to widespread disenchantment. In their view, optimists' campaigns to boost self-esteem result in people developing uncritical, unrealistic visions of their own worth, and that people with these inflated expectations are likely to face inevitable disappointment and become frustrated, angry, and cynical. Better they should not have received so much early, misleading encouragement.

Status Affluence Maintains an Unjust Social Order

There is a rather different pessimistic critique that comes, for the most part, from those on the political left. It argues that status affluence is simply an illusion, a sop, a way that elites trick ordinary folks into thinking that their lives are going well. In this vision, status affluence is a contemporary version of the bread and circuses used to keep the Roman masses amused and quiescent.

There is a long tradition of sociologists worrying about the discontents of modern life. These theorists envision a past in which people found intense satisfactions in belonging to local communities. They derived their identities—their sense of who they were—from those communities, and they had a clear sense, not just of where they belonged, but of where they fit in. People knew and respected one another as individuals, and they felt a sense of solidarity with one another. In this nostalgic view, the past becomes idealized, with people depicted as living in familiar villages, contented with their place—in time, in space, and in society.

Sociology originated in the nineteenth century, in the decades just after the Industrial Revolution, when dramatic social change seemed self-evident and troubling. People were leaving the countryside for rapidly growing cities—places that seemed more crowded, disease-ridden, and confused than their familiar villages. In those industrializing cities, they found jobs in factories—workplaces that seemed larger, crueler, and more impersonal than the fields where they had performed communal agricultural labor. Early sociologists understood that fundamental changes had been taking place, and they worried about the consequences of shifting from rural communities to bigger, more anonymous cities.

This concern has continued to shape sociological thinking. Critics warn that modern life seems to have lost many of the shared meanings that gave a sense of belonging to traditional communities. People live in cities, among people they don't know. They aren't sure where they belong, and they feel alienated, anomic, disoriented. The titles of some of sociology's all-time best sellers capture this concern with isolation—*The Lonely Crowd, The Pursuit of Loneliness,* and *Bowling Alone.*[10] Such critics particularly worry about Americans' readiness to celebrate individualism at the expense of communal solidarity.

In a sense, this critique goes, we have lost the glue—that shared sense of community—that holds social life together. In its place, we have settled for consumerism, a pursuit of an ever evolving series of trinkets—for instance, family entertainment has gone from people making music by playing instruments together in the family parlor to family members gathered around a radio, or a television, or a color TV, or, most recently, a huge flat-screen HDTV. The treadmill of technological innovation ensures that today's status symbol didn't exist yesterday and will seem passé tomorrow.

Note some features of these changes. At least in the case of home entertainment, the trend is toward passivity. Families once had to make their own entertainment, but they have become accustomed to finding amusement in sitting in front of increasingly sophisticated machines. Moreover, our world seems to become ever more individualistic; we can contrast our image of a happy, traditional family making music together against that of a family divided, with each member more likely to be a lone viewer sitting in front of a TV or monitor in his or her room. Note, too, that the process is never ending. Whatever newfangled gadget you add to your home entertainment center, it will soon become obsolete. This means that consumption becomes an endless pursuit; people rush to acquire the newest thing, only to discover that it has been replaced by some even newer status symbol. It is a system, the critics argue, that promises satisfaction but never delivers.

While critics tend to focus on the consumption of material goods as status symbols, their argument is easily extended to the general phenomenon of status affluence. Trophies, making the honor roll, gaining a top ranking, and other forms of proliferating status can be seen as just additional ways to communicate a false sense of achievement. In the critics' view, such honors are not just symbolic; they are worse than meaningless. They pit people against one another in a competition for empty honors. They promote an ideal of individualistic accomplishment while denigrating the importance of community. At the same time, such forms of status do nothing to address the fundamental class inequalities that the critics see as the central feature of modern society.

This pessimistic critique views status affluence as, at bottom, antisocial. Status affluence—both the acquisition of material status symbols and the proliferation of honors—promises what it can't deliver. As the philosophers have observed about modern life: we just can't get no satisfaction.

In sum, status affluence comes in for a good deal of criticism. It is blamed for the failings of the young (who allegedly think too well of themselves) and the disappointments of all (who find themselves condemned to community-destroying lives in individualistic pursuits for meaningless honors and materialistic consumption). It all sounds pretty grim. Should we be worried about all those prizes, valedictorians, heroes, and number-one rankings? Do they reveal some sort of underlying societal rot?

THE VALUE OF STATUS AFFLUENCE

It is remarkably easy both for optimists to praise status affluence as a cure for what ails society and for pessimists to worry that status affluence threatens to make things worse. Both critiques offer commonsense arguments that depend upon apparently reasonable assertions about how things ought to work: the optimists argue that awarding more honors will raise self-esteem and reduce inequities; the pessimists worry that too much praise damages character or induces passive acceptance of lives without true meaning. When someone makes one of these assertions forcefully enough, a lot of us nod along.

For the most part, both the optimists' and the pessimists' arguments share another quality: they emphasize the impact of status affluence *on individuals*. American culture celebrates individualism, and this individualistic focus leads us to be sympathetic to claims that highlight psychological effects. Thus, optimists emphasize the role of status in promoting self-esteem, while pessimists tend to focus on status affluence as a cause of damaged character and alienation—all arguments that emphasize the psychological impact of increased status. We are familiar with such reasoning in everyday life; we are used to explanations that focus on psychological processes—which is why both the optimists' and the pessimists' claims seem like common sense. Still, it may help to shift our focus from the individual to the social as we try to understand the meaning of status affluence.

We need to get status affluence into some sort of perspective. To begin, we might note that both the optimists' and the pessimists' arguments depend heavily upon assertion and anecdotal evidence. The optimists' insistence that boosting self-esteem offers a solution to social problems does not, as we have already noted, receive much support from researchers.

However, neither is it clear that the pessimists' fears about the decay in character—that so-called narcissism epidemic—is actually having serious consequences. Predictions that the next generation won't have what it takes have a very long history, and when we look back on the alarms of the past, they seem quaint. Once-prominent books, such as *Generation of Vipers* (1942) and *The Shook-Up Generation* (1958), are now almost forgotten.[11] The baby boomers—like the generations that preceded them—wound up living reasonably productive, reasonably conventional lives. Remember that the menace of grade inflation was first identified in 1972; the college students who were supposedly being shaped by it are now in their fifties, and we would be hard-pressed to identify just how they—or the larger society—were damaged. Perhaps we don't need to be quite so worried about the fates of Generation X, Generation Y, and so on.

Finally, there is reason to question the pessimists' critique that modern society is the setting for meaningless, alienated lives. Do contemporary people actually live the miserable, empty lives the critics describe? One surprisingly robust finding from survey research is that most Americans, when asked to assess their personal happiness, describe themselves as being pretty happy. For decades, the Gallup Poll has been asking two questions. The first is: "In general, are you satisfied or dissatisfied with the way things are going in the United States at this time?" The responses to this question fluctuate wildly over the years: in mid-October 2008 (when the scope of the recent financial crisis became glaringly evident), only 7 percent of respondents pronounced they were satisfied, whereas in February 1999 (when the dot-com bubble was still expanding), Gallup found fully 71 percent declaring themselves satisfied.[12] No real surprise: in good times people think the country's doing well, while in hard times they don't.

But compare those huge swings in public opinion with the responses to Gallup's second question: "In general, are you satisfied or dissatisfied with the way things are going in your personal life at this time?" In sharp contrast to those for the first question, the responses to this item don't fluctuate all that much. In December 2008, when it was obvious that the financial crisis was serious and likely to be prolonged, 80 percent of respondents reported that they were generally satisfied. This is a very typical response; every time Gallup has asked this question since 1979, the percentage reporting feeling satisfied has been between 73 percent (July 1979) and 87 percent (October 2000). (Moreover, among the satisfied, those who say they are "very satisfied" consistently outnumber the "somewhat satisfied" by about two to one.)[13] In other words, even when lots of people worry that the country is going to hell in a handbasket, they report feeling pretty satisfied with their own lives.

This is a fairly robust finding. For instance, since 1972, the General Social Survey has been asking respondents: "Taken all together, how would you say things are today, would you say that you are very happy, pretty happy, or not too happy?" Again, the results don't fluctuate all that much: year after year, about

30 percent of people report they are very happy; around 55 percent say they are pretty happy, and only about 15 percent choose the not-very-happy option. To be sure, happiness is shaped by other factors: those who have higher incomes, attend church, and are married are more likely to say they are very happy.[14] But the overall finding is that Americans tend to report being, not just satisfied with their lives, but actually happy.

Of course, pessimistic cultural critics may dismiss these self-evaluations, arguing—in effect—that ordinary people just don't understand that their lives lack meaning, that they actually are alienated and miserable. The people who wander through shopping malls, we are told, are deluding themselves with consumerist fantasies, imagining that they can find fulfillment by purchasing things. This is, the critics insist, an empty fantasy. People may deny that they are lonely and disenchanted, but again the critics explain that they simply don't appreciate how unhappy they actually are.

We might also wonder about the pessimists' nostalgic portrayal of the past—that vision of a meaningful, communal world we have supposedly lost. Of course, we know very little about the inner lives of preindustrial villagers, and it is easy to idealize their lot by imagining scenes such as Pieter Brueghel the Elder's familiar painting "Peasant Dance"—well-fed villagers cavorting at a festival. But that nostalgic vision ignores the high rates of infant mortality, the short life expectancies, the high levels of violence, the famines, and other less-than-ideal aspects of preindustrial life. We may like to imagine that villagers lived happy, fulfilling lives, but they certainly had plenty of reasons to feel miserable. To be sure, some late-nineteenth- and early-twentieth-century immigrants who left villages for cities complained that life was different, more impersonal, that urban life led people to forget the old ways, and the first sociologists were there to record their discontents, whereas we have few comparable records of rural peasants' lives. Certainly some of those immigrants left the cities and tried to return to their villages. But it is worth remembering that many of them stayed, not because they found the industrial world perfect, but because they saw it as the preferable option—and of course their children and the generations that followed seem to have adapted to the new environment.

In other words, the commonsense arguments made by both the optimists and the pessimists may seem convincing when we first hear them, but they assert more than they prove. Our society is certainly experiencing status affluence, but we can suspect that both the optimists' utopian visions and the pessimists' dystopian scenarios are exaggerated. Isn't there some other way— some more sociological way—to think about what's happening?

THE CENTRALITY OF SOCIAL WORLDS

Most sociologists have given status short shrift. They have paid more attention to the class system, to racial hierarchies, and— in recent decades—to gender. If we categorize people by class, race, or gender, and then compare those categories across other variables, we are likely to discover different outcomes. Thus, as has been noted, social class makes real differences in people's lives: on average, the higher people's social class, the more education they receive, the more money they make, the longer they live, and so forth. Similarly, race and gender also prove to be related to lots of variables. Class, race, and gender are revealed in broad, systematic patterns of advantage, patterns that become evident when we view society as a whole.

But that's not how most of us—most of the time—look at or experience society. We live our lives on a less grand scale, and we are more conscious of the exceptions to the rule: that guy in high school who seemed to have lots of advantages but kept messing up and never fulfilled the expectations adults had for him; and there was that other fellow, whose family wasn't well off, but who worked hard and really made something of himself. Those exceptions are why sociologists use qualifiers like "on average" or "in general" when describing social patterns. Those sociologists realize what we all know from personal experience: within the larger social patterns, there is always variation. Even privileged parents don't tell their children to relax and count on the rigid social patterns of class, race, and gender to shape their lives; rather, they tell them to work hard, because hard work pays off.

Class, race, and gender are not irrelevant to our everyday lives, but we probably spend more hours of most days thinking about status. Status becomes important at school, where children come to be considered good or poor students, and the same sorts of status judgments occur throughout life. We speak of good parents, good friends, good workers, good neighbors, and so on. When we talk this way, we're talking about respect—about status. And, most of the time, the scale is local: we know that she's a good neighbor because she is well regarded in our neighborhood; we don't turn to *U.S. News* for national rankings of neighborliness.

Status also shapes our own behavior. For the most part, we can't control our class, race, or gender, but we can affect whether we are respected and well regarded. We are used to equating status with conspicuous consumption, with people flaunting whatever today's trendy, extravagant status symbol might be;

this leads us to view the pursuit of status as ridiculous and inconsequential. But a good reputation and the esteem of others are also status symbols; all of us strive for status, not just those who spend their time collecting and flaunting expensive props.

Most status is local. We may live in a large country but, for the most part, we don't experience it as a mass society, in which each person blends into an undifferentiated mass. Rather, we spend much of our lives within smaller social worlds—in particular families, workplaces, and networks of friends, acquaintances, or other folks who share our interests in Civil War reenacting or barbershop harmonizing or whatever. Often—although by no means always—these worlds have members who share the same class, race, or gender; but each world, regardless of how advantaged or diverse its membership may be, allocates status to its members. And it is this local, intraworld status that gives people's lives much of their meaning.

So, if status is central in people's lives, what is the significance of status affluence? Focusing on the importance of status helps us see the problem with the optimists' arguments that emphasize the importance of self-esteem. Self-esteem has a psychological focus that seems intuitively reasonable in a culture that celebrates individualism. But viewed from a more sociological vantage point, status affluence can be understood as about *social* esteem: it is a way for social worlds to celebrate their values and their members' accomplishments. Similarly, the pessimists' warnings that status affluence celebrates individual triumphs at the expense of community misses the way status is produced by social worlds, for the benefit, not just of a few individual winners, but of all the members of those social worlds. Because both the optimists and the pessimists tend to assume that status affluence is something that affects individuals, they often ignore its social significance.

Why is contemporary society characterized by more status affluence? In part, this may be a response to society's larger arenas—many of us live in big cities and work for big firms. And our social worlds also can span great geographic distances. Professionals and hobbyists alike find themselves gathering in regional or even national conventions, where they can meet people who share their interests; even junior high school athletes may play on traveling teams that compete far from home. Some designation of status—an award or ranking—is a way of establishing one's place in social worlds where everyone can't possibly know everyone else. The very fact that we speak of this as "recognizing" people and their contributions or accomplishments reveals that formal status allocations are a way of compensating for our inability to readily assess the individual characters of all those we encounter.

It is worth appreciating that many awards spring from motives that are, at least in part, altruistic. It is not uncommon for individuals to endow scholarships or other honors—often in their own names or in the name of some admired (perhaps deceased) person. Each spring, for example, my university holds Honors Day, when it publishes a thick booklet, printed in a fairly small font, that lists the students who have won various scholarships and other prizes, many of which are named for either their sponsors or people those sponsors wanted to memorialize. The people who establish these prizes have found a way to link the past (those being memorialized) to the future (those who will benefit from the award). In the process, they not only recognize the award winner but also remember the person for whom the award is named. Thus, they have an opportunity to express their values and to declare that this person should not be forgotten, that some quality the person embodied ought to be honored. Far from being expressions of alienation, establishing such awards seems to be a way of expressing a sense of solidarity to a social world, if not to the larger societal whole.

Of course, when some one person wins an accolade, others do not. Hundreds of detective novels might be eligible for an award, of which dozens may be nominated, and perhaps five of the nominees are named finalists, from which one winner is chosen. Isn't there then one winner and many losers? Surely the winner must be pleased, but individualistic, psychologically focused explanations suggest that all the losers must be left disappointed, perhaps bitter, even alienated. Of course, some people do feel that way; there are what are called "bad losers." But others are considered "good losers," those who congratulate the winner, who proclaim that it is an honor just to have been in the running, just as there are "good winners" who modestly note that it was a stiff competition, that others were also deserving. Through such performances, those who win—and those who lose—can reveal their commitment to their social world's status system and its values.

Sociologists who study collective memories—the shared sense of the past held by people in various groups—often find that these memories are selective. Groups tend to tell fairly simple, coherent stories about their histories—this event was key, this individual was the central figure, and so on. It is often possible to examine the historical record and identify other events that have wound up forgotten and other people whose contributions aren't as well recalled.[15] Thus, histories of the civil rights movement often highlight the role of Rosa Parks, who was arrested after refusing to surrender her seat on a Montgomery, Alabama, bus in 1955, but those same histories usually ignore the stories of other African-American women who protested bus segregation before Parks (including one whose protest led to a favorable 1946 U.S. Supreme Court decision). We might think of those other women as contenders for collective memory; although their deeds resembled what Parks did, those women are not recalled and celebrated in the same way. Barry Schwartz, a sociologist who has analyzed how collective memory came to focus on Parks, suggests: "'Singling out' and 'setting examples,' therefore, do more than reward individuals; they perform moral functions; they provide the community with concrete exemplars of its standards, virtues, and powers."[16] A simpler story may not be accurate or complete, but it is easier to tell and easier to remember.

Something similar happens when social worlds award prizes and other forms of status to their members. Even when there is only one winner, the designation of that winner carries messages about the group—the social world—that is bestowing the honor: this is what we value; this is what we are about. Awards honor, not just the individuals who are singled out, but the world within which they act, so that, in a sense, everyone in that world is praised for being part of a worthwhile enterprise—all the world's members are, to a degree, winners. Those who don't actually win the prizes still may bask in the reflected glory.

The trend toward status affluence, then, suggests that contemporary society has found more ways to assure more people that their lives have value and meaning. Obviously, most of us have to get used to the notion that we aren't likely to receive a Nobel Prize or win an Oscar. Few of us achieve even fifteen Warholian minutes of fame on a national—let alone global—stage. Yet, within our social worlds, there are more ways of recognizing accomplishments, of passing out status boosts. Imagine a state's championship high school basketball team—the big winners, to be sure. But then there were the other teams that qualified for the state tournament (who can take pride in that achievement, even though they didn't win); and there were the players on the teams who didn't qualify for the tournament but who received athletic letters—and the players who may not have lettered but who made, or nearly made, their teams during tryouts. All of these gain some status. Status competitions rarely have one winner and lots of undifferentiated losers; more often, they provide a degree of status to lots of people. And, of course, the status ripples outward—the players' families and friends take pride in their accomplishments, as do the other students at their schools and even some of the members of their communities.

Some pessimists see this status as meaningless, as a means of placating the masses. But surely status is a central way of providing meaning, of giving individuals a sense that their social worlds make sense and have value. This occurs, not only when an individual is favored by receiving a prize or some other special recognition, but indirectly, through the experience of belonging to a world that has affirmed its values by awarding status. (Even the pessimists belong to a social world, one unified by its members' assumptions about the nature of society, and they no doubt find meaning in social criticism, allocate status within their world, find affirmation in its status system, and, one suspects, even award prizes.) Participation in social worlds provides a fundamentally social, fundamentally human experience—the sense of belonging, of having a place among others. When we think about status, it is easy to focus on its divisive qualities—the ways people flaunt status symbols to set themselves above others. But it is important to appreciate that status also fosters social cohesion—it allows individuals to locate themselves within social worlds.

Feeling connected to particular worlds should not be equated with attachments to society as a whole. Those conservatives who worry that status affluence threatens to debase society's moral standards imagine a unified social order, governed by one set of standards. But that is an unrealistic vision for any society much larger than a village. In huge, complex societies, lives are lived within social worlds, and because those worlds are diverse, we cannot be surprised that they have different standards and honor different sorts of accomplishments. Still, different standards are not an absence of standards. Most of us find meaning within our social worlds, and that meaningfulness explains the trend toward status affluence.

It is, of course, easy to make fun of self-congratulatory culture. Whenever people flaunt their statuses, we may be excused for noting that there are, with each passing year, more statuses to flaunt. When people are oblivious to this proliferation of status, when they invest their honors with more importance than observers might consider warranted, those observers may be amused—or annoyed. And certainly some status allocation is manipulative. When a fast-food franchise names an "Employee of the Month," this can be dismissed as a fairly obvious effort by management to motivate workers without actually paying them more. Yet, after we cut through all of the cynicism, a good deal of sincerity remains. Individuals often take status allocation seriously: those who are acknowledged are often pleased with the recognition, but many other people also nod and find meaning in the rituals. While it is not true that everyone wins in a society characterized by status affluence, there are at least a great many people who find reaffirmation of the meaningfulness of the social worlds they occupy.

Meaning, after all, is not absolute, but manufactured through human interaction. People decide what is disreputable and what is honorable, and in the process they come to believe in the meanings they have created. Of course, this has its comic side: people seem to fool themselves when they take their own constructions too seriously. But it is worth remembering that all we value arises from our willingness to treat the world we have created—and our actions within that world—as meaningful. Status affluence exists because it serves social ends.

NOTES

CHAPTER 1: LIFE IN AN ERA OF STATUS ABUNDANCE

1. Barone (2004: 13–14).

2. Barone (2004: 13–14).

3. Weber (1946 [1922]).

4. The classic popularized treatment of this theme is Packard (1959).

5. See Goffman (1951); Fussell (1983).

6. On lifestyles, see Weber (1946 [1922]). Analyses of high school social systems date back decades: Coleman (1961).

7. Marketing analysts have been particularly interested in classifying consumer lifestyles. One relatively recent scheme is described in Weiss (2000).

8. On statusspheres, see Wolfe (1968). On subcultures: Arnold (1970). On scenes: Irwin (1977). On fields: Bourdieu (1993); Becker and Pessin (2006). On tribes: Bennett (1999). On social worlds: Unruh (1980); Becker (1982); Becker and Pessin (2006).

9. On reenactors, see Horwitz (1998); Williams (2002).

10. Boudette (2007). For the traditionalists' views, see Barbershop Quartet Preservation Association (2008).

11. The cycle is detailed in two papers by Anselm Strauss (1982, 1984).

12. "Status by its very character involves endless struggles over the

allocation of scarce resources, especially scarce cultural resources" (Turner 1988: 9).

13. Galbraith (1958).

14. Brooks (2002: 33). Brooks has written extensively on status in contemporary social worlds; see also Brooks (2000; 2004).

15. For an argument that the social order's roots are in local arrangements, see R. Collins (2004).

16. Adler and Adler (1994); Messner (2009).

17. Such voluntary associations attracted a great deal of sociological attention through the 1950s (e.g., Gordon and Babchuk 1959), but seem to have fallen out of favor as analysts' focus began to shift toward social movements.

18. For classic statements on this theme, see Rosenberg and White (1957).

19. Turow (1997).

20. For an early discussion of the link between consumer choice and lifestyle diversity, see Toffler (1970). For a more recent treatment, see Weiss (2000).

21. Bourdieu (1984).

22. Ward (1996).

23. Brooks (2004: 73).

24. Cerulo (2006) views the emphasis on awards and other positive statuses as part of a broader cultural tendency to emphasize what is positive, rather than negative.

25. On symbolic inflation, see Klapp (1991).

CHAPTER 2: PRIZE PROLIFERATION

1. Complete lists of past award winners can be found at the websites of the Mystery Writers of America (2009) and the Crime Writers' Association (2009).

2. Many winners of other mystery awards included in figure 1 are cataloged at the Omnimystery website (Omnimystery 2009): Best Books Awards (*USA Book News;* two mystery awards, established 2006); British Book Industry Award (one mystery award, 2005); the David Award (Deadly Ink Press; one award, 2007); Dilys Award (Independent

Mystery Booksellers Association; one award, 1992); ForeWord Book of the Year (*ForeWord Magazine;* three mystery awards—gold, silver, bronze, 2000); Benjamin Franklin Award (Independent Book Publishers Association; one mystery award, 2001); Hammett Prize (International Association of Crime Writers; one award, 1991); IPPY Awards (*Independent Publisher;* two mystery awards—gold, silver, 2001); Lambda Awards (Lambda Literary Foundation; two awards—best gay and best lesbian mysteries, 1988); *Los Angeles Times* Book Prize (one mystery award, 2001); Next Generation Indie Book Award (one mystery award, 2008); Premier Book Award (one mystery award, 2008); the now-defunct Quill Award (Quills Literary Foundation; one mystery award, 2005–7); Reviewers Choice Awards (*Romantic Times Book Reviews;* 6 mystery awards, 1999); Spotted Owl Award (Friends of Mystery; one award, 1996); Thriller Awards (International Thriller Writers; three awards, 2006). Other awards were located independently from the sources cited: Agatha Awards (Malice Domestic 2009); Anthony Awards (Bouchercon World Mystery Convention 2009); Barry Awards (six awards, 1997; *Deadly Pleasures* 2009); Derringer Awards (Short Mystery Fiction Society 2009); Gumshoe Awards (five awards, 2002; Mystery Ink 2009); the now-defunct Herodotus Awards (for historical mysteries, six awards, 1998–2000; Historical Mystery Appreciation Society 2009); Lovey Awards (nine awards, 2000; Love Is Murder 2009); Macavity Awards (Mystery Readers International 2009); Nero Wolfe Awards (Wolfe Pack 2009); Shamus Awards (Private Eye Writers of America 2009); Theakston's Award (one award, 2005; Harrogate Crime Writing Festival 2009). In years when an award had two or more different recipients, figure 1 counts each recipient as a separate award.

3. The *Locus* Index to Science Fiction Awards (Kelly 2009) offers a thorough overview for that genre. There does not seem to be an equivalent summary for romance fiction prizes, but prominent award programs are sponsored by the Romance Writers of America (2009), the Romantic Novelists' Association (2009), *Romantic Times* magazine (2009), the ParaNormalRomance Groups (2009), Christian publishers (Christy Awards 2009), and so on. On sociology prizes, see Best (2008). On book and film awards, see English (2005: 323–28).

4. *Baseball Almanac* (2009).

5. On honorary degrees, see Cronin (2002). On Marine Corps medals, see Mugno (1994). On Army medals, see Stone (1999: 1A). On the Iowa State Fair blue ribbons, see Sutherland (2003: 308–9). On bowl games, see College Football Poll (2010). "Trophy creep" comes from Dickinson (2005). On Malaysia, see Ngah (1995). On science prize competitions, see Hotz (2009); McKinsey and Company (2009).

6. Goode (1978: 164); English (2005: 17). See also Horowitz (1987); Zuckerman (1992).

7. There are manuals for would-be prize givers: Leverence (1997); McKinsey and Company (2009).

8. On the mechanics of the Nobel Prize, see Feldman (2000). In the United Kingdom, awards for literary fiction and other arts prizes have become popular spectacles; each televised awards ceremony is the centerpiece of prolonged media coverage, first speculating about who may win, then evaluating the choice once it has been revealed. See Todd (1996); English (2005); Street (2005).

9. Thomson (2008: M3).

10. On prizes as an expression of groups' values, see Goode (1978: 163–71). On PETA, see Hotz (2009).

11. English (2005: 64); Hotz (2009); McKinsey and Company (2009).

12. On poetry awards, see English (2001); Bartlett (2005); Alpaugh (2010). On halls of fame: James (1994); Danilov (1997).

13. Leverence (1997).

14. English (2005). For Dagger sponsors, see Crime Writers' Association (2009).

15. Zuckerman (1977: 196–200).

16. English (2005: 237–46). On prize recipients' awareness of criticism about the politics of prize giving and some of their strategies for avoiding being the targets of envy, see Heinich (2009).

17. Albergotti (2007).

18. "Gedunk is a traditional navy term, and it refers to the ship's store which sells candies, cigarettes, toiletries, and 'incidentals,' and/or the actual candies and incidentals themselves. Using the term in reference to war medals represents an obvious attempt to trivialize and ridicule the medals" (Johnson 2008). On Vietnam veterans: *New*

York Times (1971). On British recipients denouncing sponsors' activities: Todd (1996); English (2005).

19. McPhedran (2003).

20. DeOliveira (2000: 104). More generally: "Such enhancement [through an award] for the individual member affirms the importance of good performance for all others in the role.... In the process, the organization itself garners credit for the individual's accomplishment" (Trice 1985: 249).

21. On Nobel-like awards, see English (2005: 61; brackets in original). On the Stockholm Prize, see *Criminologist* (2005: 5). On status consideration in proposing new prizes, see Street (2005).

22. Goode (1978); Strauss (1982).

23. Goode (1978: 175).

24. On college honor societies, see Current (1990); Luebke (2001); Association of College Honor Societies (2009). Phi Beta Kappa's failure to join the ACHS resembles the Nobel Foundation's unwillingness to participate in the International Congress of Distinguished Awards. According to English, in the Nobel Foundation's view, "the function of the IDCA would be to secure and defend the upper tier of the awards pyramid—the tier, that is, just below the untouchable pinnacle on which the Nobel alone resides" (2005: 62). See Hu (2010) on high school honor societies, and National Association of Elementary School Principals (2008) on the NEHS. On halls of fame: Danilov (1997); Rubin (1997).

25. Tilly (2008).

26. On ethnic prizes, see King-O'Riain (2006). For an argument that special prizes ought to be established for women, see Hall and Sandler (1982). On doubts about having separate award systems for men and women, see Riding (2005).

27. Zangen (2003).

28. Cieply (2009: C1); Akbar (2010).

29. Bruin (1987).

30. Stone (1999: 1A).

31. Bender (2003: A1); Hooper (2009: A19).

32. Nyhan (1997); Stout (2000).

33. Borch (2006: 6).

34. On honorary degrees, see Cronin (2002: 61–62). On cultural inflation, see Gabler (2010). On the Marine Corps, see Mugno (1994: 77). On inflationary processes, see Klapp (1991).

35. Mugno (1994: 83); see also Marine (2004); Black Beret (2005).

36. For arguments that military medals are not given too freely, see Marshall (1953); Newman (1967). These articles respond to critics of medal inflation during the wars in Korea and Vietnam; I have not seen parallel comments for more recent wars, perhaps because inflation's critics seem to have gained little traction.

37. On inertia as a social force, see Becker (1995).

38. Mugno (1994: 80).

39. On the Congressional Medal of Honor, see *Associated Press Online* (2005). On Harvard, see Hartocollis (2002).

40. Bernstein (1996).

CHAPTER 3: HONORING STUDENTS

1. For a statistical overview of American education, see National Center for Education Statistics (2008).

2. Ravitch (2000: 465). Other prominent statements of the mastery position include Bloom (1987) and Hirsch (2006).

3. Flesch (1955: 2); National Commission on Excellence in Education (1983: 5).

4. Other analysts have developed distinctions that parallel my categories of mastery and opportunity. For instance, in "On the Conflict of Social Philosophies in Higher Education," Martin E. Spencer (1979) contrasts a Philosophy of Merit with a Philosophy of Right. David F. Larabee (1997: 7) suggests: "High schools in the United States today are characterized by a continuing rhetorical commitment to the merit principle but a set of educational practices (such as social promotion) that are antimeritocratic."

5. For examples of analyses that emphasize the importance of schools' providing opportunities, see Noguera (2003); Carter (2005); and Kozol (2005).

6. On the rejection of red ink for grading, see Aoki (2004). On restrictions on playground games, see Labash (2001); Cowan (2007).

7. For an illustration of how cultural capital shapes the lives of children, as well as an introduction to the concept, see Lareau (2003). On the concept's origins, see Bourdieu (1984).

8. Gouras (2004).

9. Orrin Klapp (1991: 112) suggests that spreading honors widely is one consequence of egalitarianism: "an ideology stressing equality of men will favor as many as possible having (at least access to) the same number and kinds of valuable symbols."

10. Ravitch (2000: 465).

11. Like other institutions in our society, schools continually establish new social worlds—new programs of instruction, new student organizations, and the like—and these new worlds often see the creation of awards for excellence as a means of legitimating their activities. See Strauss (1982).

12. I. Peterson (1972: 21).

13. Mansfield (2001: B24); Kohn (2002: B7). On rival data sets: Stuart Rojstaczer maintains the website Gradeinflation.com (2009), which presents data from 170 U.S. colleges and universities, suggesting that the average GPA rose from 2.93 in 1991–92 to 3.11 in 2006–7; however, Clifford Adelman (2004) suggests that national surveys of grade cohorts show little change since the 1970s.

14. On the Monitoring the Future data, see Twenge and Campbell (2008: 1084). On weighting advanced classes, see Lang (2007).

15. Marquardt (2009).

16. These have inspired bumper stickers featuring satirical counterclaims: e.g., "My kid sells term papers to your honor student"; "My Kid Was Prisoner of the Month at Orange County Jail" (BumperArt .com 2009).

17. Behrendt (1988); Hu (2010).

18. Mathews (1997: J1). On multiple valedictorians, see also Glod (2006); Lang (2007).

19. Horswell (2005: B4); Talbot (2005).

20. Mathews (1997: J1).

21. Fuetsch and Chalmers (2004).

22. Lee (2005).

23. Shulleeta (2008); Warren, Grodsky, and Lee (2008: 102, 101).

24. For instance, Mathews (2007) defends honors courses against suggestions that they are no longer needed in high schools with AP programs. He argues that the honors option provides important opportunities for less advantaged students who may not qualify for AP courses.

25. Brooks (2007: A25). See also Adler and Adler (1994); Lareau (2003); Messner (2009).

26. Schemo (2009).

27. For kindergarten gear, see GraduationSource.com (2009). Hoffman (2008: ST1) quotes Obama in discussing competing claims about eighth-grade graduations.

28. R. Collins (1979); Larabee (1997).

29. Barone (2004).

30. Just (1970); Sarkesian (1975).

31. Sarkesian (1975: 68); Dilworth (1971: 1); Mugno (1994: 73).

32. Sarkesian (1975: 72). See also Mugno (1994); Stone (1999).

33. On title inflation, see Dawson (2009).

CHAPTER 4: EVERYDAY HEROES

1. For information on the Purina Animal Hall of Fame, see Purina (2009). Minnesota offers an example of a program maintained by a state veterinary association (Minnesota Veterinary Medical Association 2009).

2. Raglan (1936: 179–80).

3. Carlyle (1993 [1841]: 13).

4. Klapp's book by that title appeared in 1962. We can suspect that, had he waited just a few years, changes in public discourse might have caused him to identify a fourth category—victims (Best 1999).

5. Klapp (1962: 31).

6. Klapp (1962: 46–47).

7. Klapp (1962: 96, 143).

8. Edelstein (1996: 5, 4).

9. Furedi (1997: 64). On the notion of risk society, see Beck (1992).

10. Berkowitz (1987); Edelstein (1996).

11. On military heroism, see Anderson (1986); Riemer (1998). On the Congressional Medal of Honor, see Blake (1973); Blake and Butler (1976).

12. Carnegie Hero Fund Commission (2009).

13. Contrast, for example, Radford (2005) and Wieting (2000).

14. CNN (2009).

15. Berkowitz (1987: xi).

16. My Hero Project (2009).

17. Busch Entertainment Corporation (2009).

18. K. Peterson (2007).

19. Firefighter Angel Stickers (2009).

20. Gantenbein (2003).

21. On the New York firefighters' moral currency, see Monahan (2010). On the mine disaster, see Kitch (2007).

22. Perez-Pena (2007: B1).

23. Reagan (1981).

24. McInerney (2006: 660, 659).

25. Furedi (1997: 12).

26. Sontag (1978).

27. Seale (1995: 602, 606). See also Seale (2002).

28. Porpora (1996).

29. Holub, Trask, and Mullins (2008: 570).

30. Gibson et al. (2007).

31. Schuman, Schwartz, and D'Arcy (2005); Kubal (2008). For a more general statement of the problem, see Fine (2001).

32. Edelstein (1996).

33. *Washington Times* (2003).

34. DeLong (2007).

35. *New York Times* (2008). For a detailed analysis of the media coverage about Jessica Lynch and Pat Tillman, see Krakauer (2009).

36. For an overview of the case, see Robin (2004: 57–84).

37. Kirkpatrick (2003: 13); see also Meyer (1990); Kurtz (2003).

38. Rutenberg (2004: 8); see also Romano (2004). A parallel case occurred when congressional representative John Murtha—also a decorated veteran—challenged Iraq policy; his opponents began questioning the basis for his medals. See Kurtz and Murray (2006).

39. Hackworth (2004: 15A); Fackler (2004).

40. Roberts (2002).

41. *Oxford English Dictionary* (2009).

42. Thus, the occasional bickering about whether the economics prize (officially the Sveriges Risbank Prize in Economic Sciences in Memory of Alfred Nobel) is a "real" Nobel Prize.

CHAPTER 5: RANKING AND RATING

1. *Consumer Reports* (1986).

2. Rotten Tomatoes (2009); Motion Picture Association of America (2009).

3. Cerulo (2006: 110).

4. Zuckerman (1977: 196–200).

5. For examples of how lifestyles are shaped by patterns of choices, see Weiss (2000).

6. For a thorough discussion of how those making evaluations can convince others of their credibility, see Blank (2007).

7. Blank (2007) also offers a detailed discussion of various methods for rating and ranking.

8. Tugend (2007).

9. On the tendency to assume numbers are meaningful, see Best (2001, 2004).

10. Motion Picture Association of America (2009).

11. On the campaign against comic books, see Nyberg (1998) and Hajdu (2008). On the campaign leading to record labels, see Gray (1989).

12. For the interns' accounts, see Farber (1972); Renold (1975).

13. Blank (2007: 79).

14. Meredith (2004).

15. Tuchman (2009) discusses how administrators at "Wannabe U"

(an institution that aspires to improve its reputation) calculate how they can best boost their rankings.

16. Sauder (2006).

17. McCormick (2007).

18. Hess and Gift (2009).

19. For the 2008 formula, see *U.S. News & World Report* (2008).

20. *Inside Higher Ed* (2010).

21. *Inside Higher Ed* (2009b).

22. Espeland and Sauder (2009: 19).

23. Espeland and Sauder (2007: 31).

24. Bastedo and Bowman (2010).

25. *Inside Higher Ed* (2009a).

26. Sauder and Fine (2008).

27. Sauder (2006); Sauder and Lancaster (2006).

28. The formula in effect when this was written may be found at Morse and Flanigan (2009).

29. Sauder (2006); Sauder and Lancaster (2006); Espeland and Sauder (2007).

30. Myers (2007: B7).

31. *Inside Higher Ed* (2007a).

32. *Inside Higher Ed* (2007b).

33. *Washington Monthly* (2006).

34. *Washington Monthly* (2007).

35. Goldin (2006).

36. Rosenfeld and Lauritsen (2008: 66).

CHAPTER 6: THE SIGNIFICANCE OF CONGRATULATORY CULTURE

1. Galbraith (1958).

2. On the rise and spread of the idea of self-esteem, see Ward (1996) and Hewitt (1998).

3. For suggestions for play, see Plummer (2007). For the classroom, see Lawrence (2006).

4. Clayton (2007); C. Collins (2007); Zaslow (2007).

5. Greenberger et al. (2008).

6. Reynolds et al. (2006: 187, 201).

7. Twenge and Campbell (2009: 13, 277).

8. Henderlong and Lepper (2002: 791, 779, 782).

9. Baumeister et al. (2003: 39).

10. Riesman (1950); Slater (1970); Putnam (2000).

11. Wylie (1942); Salisbury (1958).

12. *Gallup Poll* (2009: "Satisfaction with the United States").

13. *Gallup Poll* (2009: "Satisfaction with Personal Life").

14. Pew Research Center (2006).

15. For examples of selective collective memories, see Armstrong and Crage (2006); Schwartz (2009).

16. Schwartz (2009: 135).

REFERENCES

Adelman, Clifford. 2004. *Principal Indicators of Student Academic Histories in Postsecondary Education, 1972–2000.* Washington, DC: U.S. Department of Education, Institute of Education Sciences.

Adler, Patricia A., and Peter Adler. 1994. "Social Reproduction and the Corporate Other: The Institutionalization of Afterschool Activities." *Sociological Quarterly* 35: 309–28.

Akbar, Arifa. 2010. "Judges to Name Winner of 'Lost' Booker Prize." *The Independent,* February 1, 18.

Albergotti, Reed. 2007. "How to Win a Marathon." *Wall Street Journal,* June 23, 1.

Alpaugh, David. 2010. "The New Math of Poetry." *Chronicle of Higher Education,* February 26, B12–B14.

Anderson, Jeffrey W. 1986. "Military Heroism: An Occupational Definition." *Armed Forces and Society* 12: 591–606.

Aoki, Naomi. 2004. "Harshness of Red Marks Has Students Seeing Purple." *Boston Globe,* August 23, A1.

Armstrong, Elizabeth A., and Suzanna M. Crage. 2006. "Movements and Memory: The Making of the Stonewall Myth." *American Sociological Review* 71: 724–51.

Arnold, David O., ed. 1970. *The Sociology of Subcultures.* Berkeley, CA: Glendessary.

Associated Press Online. 2005. "House Votes to Tighten Rules on Awards." (January 26).

Association of College Honor Societies. 2009. www.achsnatl.org (retrieved June 24, 2009).

Barbershop Quartet Preservation Association. 2008. www.bqpa.com (retrieved July 9, 2008)

Barone, Michael. 2004. *Hard America, Soft America: Competition vs. Coddling and the Battle for the Nation's Future.* New York: Crown.

Bartlett, Thomas. 2005. "Rhyme and Unreason." *Chronicle of Higher Education,* May 20, A12–A14.

Baseball Almanac. 2009. "Baseball Awards." www.baseball-almanac.com (retrieved December 14, 2009).

Bastedo, Michael N., and Nicholas A. Bowman. 2010. "*U.S. News & World Report* College Rankings: Modeling Institutional Effects on Organizational Reputation." *American Journal of Education* 116: 163–83.

Baumeister, Roy F., Jennifer D. Campbell, Joachim I. Krueger, and Kathleen D. Vohs. 2003. "Does High Self-Esteem Cause Better Performance, Interpersonal Success, Happiness, or Healthier Lifestyles?" *Psychological Science in the Public Interest* 4: 1–44.

Beck, Ulrich. 1992. *Risk Society: Towards a New Modernity.* London: Sage.

Becker, Howard S. 1982. *Art Worlds.* Berkeley: University of California Press.

———. 1995. "The Power of Inertia." *Qualitative Sociology* 18: 301–9.

Becker, Howard S., and Alain Pessin. 2006. "A Dialogue on the Ideas of 'World' and 'Field.'" *Sociological Forum* 21: 275–86.

Behrendt, Barbara. 1988. "Stickers Boost Academic Work." *St. Petersburg* [FL] *Times (Citrus Times),* January 17, 1.

Bender, Bryan. 2003. "Fast, Furious Wars Mean Fewer Medals." *Boston Globe,* May 25, A1.

Bennett, Andy. 1999. "Subcultures or Neo-Tribes?: Rethinking the Relationship Between Youth, Style and Musical Taste." *Sociology* 33: 599–617.

Berkowitz, Bill. 1987. *Local Heroes.* Lexington, MA: Lexington Books.

Bernstein, Emily M. 1996. "Phi Beta Kappa Key Being Turned Down by Many Honorees." *New York Times,* May 26, 1.

Best, Joel. 1999. *Random Violence: How We Talk about New Crimes and New Victims*. Berkeley: University of California Press.

———. 2001. *Damned Lies and Statistics: Untangling Numbers from the Media, Politicians, and Activists*. Berkeley: University of California Press.

———. 2004. *More Damned Lies and Statistics: How Numbers Confuse Public Issues*. Berkeley: University of California Press.

———. 2008. "Prize Proliferation." *Sociological Forum* 23: 1–27.

Black Beret. 2005. "The Latest on the Black Beret." www.rangerblackberet.com (retrieved September 7, 2005).

Blake, Joseph A. 1973. "The Congressional Medal of Honor in Three Wars." *Pacific Sociological Review* 16: 166–76.

Blake, Joseph A., and Suellen Butler. 1976. "The Medal of Honor, Combat Orientations and Latent Role Structure in the United States Military." *Sociological Quarterly* 17: 561–67.

Blank, Grant. 2007. *Critics, Ratings, and Society: The Sociology of Reviews*. Lanham, MD: Rowman & Littlefield.

Bloom, Allan. 1987. *The Closing of the American Mind*. New York: Simon & Schuster.

Borch, Fred L. 2006. "'Wounded in Action': The Curious History of Combat Injuries Qualifying for the Purple Heart." *Journal of the Orders and Medals Society of America* 57 (March-April): 2–18.

Bouchercon World Mystery Convention. 2009. "Anthony Awards." www.bouchercon.info/history.html (retrieved June 24, 2009).

Boudette, Neal E. 2007. "Quartets Contend with Disharmony in the Barbershop." *Wall Street Journal*, July 2, A1.

Bourdieu, Pierre. 1984. *Distinction: A Social Critique of the Judgement of Taste*. Cambridge, MA: Harvard University Press.

———. 1993. *The Field of Cultural Production*. New York: Columbia University Press.

Brooks, David. 2000. *Bobos in Paradise: The New Upper Class and How They Got There*. New York: Simon & Schuster.

———. 2002. "Superiority Complex." *Atlantic Monthly* 290 (November): 32–33.

————. 2004. *On Paradise Drive: How We Live Now (And Always Have) in the Future Tense*. New York: Simon & Schuster.

————. 2007. "The National Pastime." *New York Times,* June 15, A25.

Bruin, K. 1987. "Distinction and Democratization: Royal Decorations in the Netherlands." *Netherlands Journal of Sociology* 23: 17–30.

BumperArt.com. 2009. "Honor Student . . . Bumper Stickers and Small Stickers." www.bumperart.com (retrieved November 28, 2009).

Busch Entertainment Corporation. 2009. "Here's to the Heroes." www.herosalute.com/cavatx/index.html (retrieved May 31, 2009).

Carlyle, Thomas. 1993 [1841]. *On Heroes, Hero-Worship, and the Heroic in History*. Berkeley: University of California Press.

Carnegie Hero Fund Commission. 2009. www.carnegiehero.org (retrieved May 26, 2009).

Carter, Prudence L. 2005. *Keepin' It Real: School Success Beyond Black and White*. New York: Oxford University Press.

Cerulo, Karen A. 2006. *Never Saw It Coming: Cultural Challenges to Envisioning the Worst*. Chicago: University of Chicago Press.

Christy Awards. 2009. www.Christyawards.com (retrieved June 24, 2009).

Cieply, Michael. 2009. "Academy Expands Best-Picture Pool to 10." *New York Times,* June 25, C1.

Clayton, Victoria. 2007. "Are We Raising a Nation of Little Egomaniacs?" *MSNBC.com* (April 2). www.msnbc.msn.com (retrieved April 2, 2007).

CNN. 2009. *CNN Heroes*. www.cnn.com/SPECIALS/cnn.heroes/ (retrieved May 26, 2009).

Coleman, James Samuel. 1961. *The Adolescent Society*. New York: Free Press.

College Football Poll. 2010. "College Football Bowl Games." www.collegefootballpoll.com (retrieved February 7, 2010).

Collins, Clayton. 2007. "Has Generation Y Overdosed on Self-Esteem?" *Christian Science Monitor,* March 2, 1.

Collins, Randall. 1979. *The Credential Society: An Historical Sociology of Education and Stratification*. New York: Academic Press.

————. 2004. *Interaction Ritual Chains*. Princeton, NJ: Princeton University Press.

Consumer Reports. 1986. *I'll Buy That! 50 Small Wonders and Big Deals That Revolutionized the Lives of Consumers*. Mount Vernon, NY: Consumers Union.

Cowan, Alison Leigh. 2007. "School Recess Gets Gentler, and the Adults Are Dismayed." *New York Times*, December 14, B1.

Crime Writers' Association. 2009. www.thecwa.co.uk (retrieved June 24, 2009).

Criminologist. 2005. "Stockholm Prize in Criminology." 30 (September): 5.

Cronin, Blaise. 2002. "Honoris Causa." *Academic Questions* 16: 60–68.

Current, Richard Nelson. 1990. *Phi Beta Kappa in American Life: The First Two Hundred Years*. New York: Oxford University Press.

Danilov, Victor J. 1997. *Hall of Fame Museums: A Reference Guide*. Westport, CT: Greenwood.

Dawson, Dudley B. 2009. "Job Title Inflation, Part 1: Job Title Inflation Reaches Alarming Levels." *San Francisco Examiner*. www.examiner.com (retrieved June 17, 2009).

Deadly Pleasures. 2009. "Barry Awards." www.deadlypleasures.com/barry (retrieved June 24, 2009).

Delong, Michael. 2007. "Politics During Wartime." *New York Times*, April 27, 27.

DeOliveira, Sandi Michele. 2000. "Whose Prize Is It Anyway? Press Coverage of the 1998 Nobel Prize-Winner for Literature." Pp. 101–11 in *Advertising and Identity in Europe: The I of the Beholder*, edited by Jackie Cannon, Patricia Anne Odber de Baubeta, and Robin Warner. Portland, OR: Intellect.

Dickinson, Amy. 2005. "Ask Amy." *Chicago Tribune*, December 1.

Dilworth, Robert M. 1971. "Efficiency Report Inflation: A Comparative Analysis of U.S. Army and Selected Foreign Officer Evaluation Systems." Unpublished master's thesis, U.S. Army Command and General Staff College.

Edelstein, Alan. 1996. *Everybody Is Sitting on the Curb: How and Why America's Heroes Disappeared*. Westport, CT: Praeger.

English, James F. 2001. "Prizes." Pp. 579–83 in *Encyclopedia of American Poetry: The Twentieth Century,* edited by Eric L. Haralson. Chicago: Fitzroy Dearborn.

————. 2005. *The Economy of Prestige: Prizes, Awards, and the Circulation of Cultural Value.* Cambridge, MA: Harvard University Press.

Espeland, Wendy Nelson, and Michael Sauder. 2007. "Rankings and Reactivity: How Public Measures Recreate Social Worlds." *American Journal of Sociology* 113: 1–40.

————. 2009. "Rating the Rankings." *Contexts* 8 (Spring): 16–21.

Fackler, Martin L. 2004. "Trying to Acquire Purple Hearts." *Washington Times,* August 26, A10.

Farber, Stephen. 1972. *The Movie Rating Game.* Washington: Public Affairs Press.

Feldman, Burton. 2000. *The Nobel Prize: The History of Genius, Controversy, and Prestige.* New York: Arcade.

Fine, Gary Alan. 2001. *Difficult Reputations: Collective Memories of the Evil, Inept, and Controversial.* Chicago: University of Chicago Press.

Firefighter Angel Stickers. 2009. www.zazzle.com (retrieved November 18, 2009).

Flesch, Rudolf. 1955. *Why Johnny Can't Read, and What You Can Do about It.* New York: Harper & Row.

Fuetsch, Michele, and Mike Chalmers. 2004. "Do 3-tiered Diplomas Resegregate Our Kids?" *Wilmington* [DE] *New Journal,* April 25.

Furedi, Frank. 1997. *Culture of Fear: Risk-Taking and the Morality of Low Expectation.* New York: Continuum.

Fussell, Paul. 1983. *Class: A Guide to the American Status System.* New York: Summit.

Gabler, Neal. 2010. "An Oscar 'Panderocracy.'" *Los Angeles Times,* January 17. www.latimes.com (retrieved March 8, 2010).

Galbraith, John Kenneth. 1958. *The Affluent Society.* Boston: Houghton Mifflin.

Gallup Poll. 2009. "Topics A to Z." www.gallup.com/poll/Topics.aspx ?CSTS=wwwsitemap&to=POLL-Topics-A-to-Z (retrieved July 29, 2009).

Gantenbein, Douglas. 2003. "Smoke and Mirrors: Stop Calling Firefighters 'Heroes.'" *Slate.com* (October 31). www.slate.com/id/2090573 (retrieved May 31, 2009).

Gibson, Gregory C., Richard Hogan, John Stahura, and Eugene Jackson. 2007. "The *Making* of Heroes: An Attributional Perspective." *Sociological Focus* 40: 72–97.

Glod, Maria. 2006. "High Schools Make Room at Top for Grads." *Washington Post,* June 17, A1.

Goffman, Erving. 1951. "Symbols of Class Status." *British Journal of Sociology* 2: 294–304.

Goldin, Rebecca. 2006. "College Rankings Mania: *The Washington Monthly*'s Bizarre Best College List." *Statistical Assessment Service* (August 29). http://stats.org (retrieved May 16, 2007).

Goode, William J. 1978. *The Celebration of Heroes: Prestige as a Control System.* Berkeley: University of California Press.

Gordon, C. Wayne, and Nicholas Babchuk. 1959. "A Typology of Voluntary Associations." *American Sociological Review* 24: 265–73.

Gouras, Matt. 2004. "School Honor Rolls Under Privacy Scrutiny." *Las Vegas Sun,* January 24. www.lasvegassun.com (retrieved January 24, 2004).

Gradeinflation.com. 2009. www.gradeinflation.com (retrieved March 12, 2009).

GraduationSource.com. 2009. "Kindergarten Graduation Cap, Gown, Tassel, Diploma, & Ring Package." www.graduationsource.com (retrieved June 23, 2009).

Gray, Herman. 1989. "Popular Music as a Social Problem." Pp. 143–58 in *Images of Issues: Typifying Contemporary Social Problems,* edited by Joel Best. Hawthorne, NY: Aldine de Gruyter.

Greenberger, Ellen, Jared Lessard, Chuansheng Chen, and Susan P. Farruggia. 2008. "Self-Entitled College Students: Contributions of Personality, Parenting, and Motivational Factors." *Journal of Youth and Adolescence* 37: 1193–1204.

Hackworth, David H. 2004. "The Meaning of a Purple Heart." *USA Today,* June 16, 15A.

Hajdu, David. 2008. *The Ten-Cent Plague: The Great Comic-Book Scare and How It Changed America.* New York: Farrar, Straus and Giroux.

Hall, Roberta M., and Bernice Resnick Sandler. 1982. "Women Winners." Report ED231249, Project on the Status and Education of Women, Association of American Colleges.

Harrogate Crime Writing Festival. 2009. "Theakstons' Old Peculier Crime Novel of the Year." www.harrogate-festival.org/crime/award (retrieved June 24, 2009).

Hartocollis, Anemona. 2002. "Harvard Faculty Votes to Put the Excellence Back in the A." *New York Times,* May 22, A20.

Heinich, Nathalie. 2009. "The Sociology of Vocational Prizes: Recognition as Esteem." *Theory, Culture and Society* 26: 85–107.

Henderlong, Jennifer, and Mark R. Lepper. 2002. "The Effects of Praise on Children's Intrinsic Motivation: A Review and Synthesis." *Psychological Bulletin* 128: 774–95.

Hess, Frederick M., and Thomas Gift. 2009. "Beware College Rankings." *National Review Online* (March 23). www.nationalreview.com (retrieved March 23, 2009).

Hewitt, John P. 1998. *The Myth of Self-Esteem: Finding Happiness and Solving Problems in America.* New York: St. Martin's.

Hirsch, E. D., Jr. 2006. *The Knowledge Deficit: Closing the Shocking Education Gap for American Children.* Boston: Houghton Mifflin.

Historical Mystery Appreciation Society. 2009. www.themysterybox.com/hmas (retrieved 2009).

Hoffman, Jan. 2008. "Does 8th-Grade Pomp Fit the Circumstance?" *New York Times,* June 22, ST1.

Holub, Shayla C., Marie S. Trask, and David Mullins. 2008. "Gender Differences in Children's Hero Attributions." *Sex Roles* 58: 567–78.

Hooper, Ed. 2009. "Leave the Medal of Honor Alone." *Washington Post,* October 1, A19.

Horowitz, Irving Louis. 1987. "Publishing and Prizing." *Book Research Quarterly* 3 (Winter): 18–21.

Horswell, Cindy. 2005. "Senior at Top of Class Offered 'Honorary' Title." *Houston Chronicle,* May 17, B4.

Horwitz, Tony. 1998. *Confederates in the Attic: Dispatches from the Unfinished Civil War.* New York: Pantheon.

Hotz, Robert Lee. 2009. "The Science Prize: Innovation or Stealth Advertising?" *Wall Street Journal,* May 8, A9.

Hu, Winnie. 2010. "As Honor Students Multiply, Who Really Is One?" *New York Times,* January 1, A1.

Inside Higher Ed. 2007a. "Refusing to Rank." (August 17). www.inside highered.com (retrieved August 21, 2007).

———. 2007b. "Watered Down Call for Rankings Reform." (September 10). www.insidehighered.com (retrieved September 11, 2007).

———. 2009a. "The Best University?" (June 9). www.insidehighered .com (retrieved June 9, 2009).

———. 2009b. "'Manipulating,' Er, Influencing *U.S. News.*" (June 3). www.insidehighered.com (retrieved June 3, 2009).

———. 2010. "You Think We're Rankings-Obsessed?" (February 1). www.insidehighered.com (retrieved February 6, 2010).

Irwin, John. 1977. *Scenes.* Beverly Hills, CA: Sage.

James, Bill. 1994. *The Politics of Glory: How Baseball's Hall of Fame Really Works.* New York: Macmillan.

Johnson, John M. 2008. "My Short and Happy Life as a Decorated War Hero." *Studies in Symbolic Interaction* 30: 325–34.

Just, Ward. 1970. *Military Men.* New York: Knopf.

Kelly, Mark R. 2009. "The *Locus* Index to Science Fiction Awards." www.locusmag.com/SFAwards/Index (retrieved June 24, 2009).

King-O'Riain, Rebecca Chiyoko. 2006. *Pure Beauty: Judging Race in Japanese American Beauty Pageants.* Minneapolis: University of Minnesota Press.

Kirkpatrick, David D. 2003. "Pulitzer Board Won't Void '32 Award to *Times* Writer." *New York Times,* November 22, 13.

Kitch, Carolyn. 2007. "Mourning 'Men Joined in Peril and Purpose': Working-Class Heroism in News Repair of the Sago Miners' Story." *Critical Studies in Media Communication* 24: 115–31.

Klapp, Orrin E. 1962. *Heroes, Villains, and Fools: The Changing American Character.* Englewood Cliffs, NJ: Prentice-Hall.

———. 1991. *Inflation of Symbols: Loss of Values in American Culture.* New Brunswick, NJ: Transaction.

Kohn, Alfie. 2002. "The Dangerous Myth of Grade Inflation." *Chronicle of Higher Education,* November 8, B7.

Kozol, Jonathan. 2005. *The Shame of the Nation: The Restoration of Apartheid Schooling in America.* New York: Crown.

Krakauer, Jon. 2009. *Where Men Win Glory: The Odyssey of Pat Tillman.* New York: Doubleday.

Kubal, Timothy. 2008. *Cultural Movements and Collective Memory: Christopher Columbus and the Rewriting of the National Origin Myth.* New York: Palgrave Macmillan.

Kurtz, Howard. 2003. "*N.Y. Times* Agrees 1932 Pulitzer Prize Was Not Deserved." *New York Times,* October 23, C8.

Kurtz, Howard, and Shailagh Murray. 2006. "Web Site Attacks Critic of War: Opponents Question Murtha's Medals." *Washington Post,* January 14, A5.

Labash, Matt. 2001. "What's Wrong with Dodgeball?" *Weekly Standard,* June 25, 17–25.

Lang, David M. 2007. "Class Rank, GPA, and Valedictorians: How High Schools Rank Students." *American Secondary Education* 35 (Spring): 36–48.

Larabee, David F. 1997. *How to Succeed in School Without Really Learning: The Credentials Race in American Education.* New Haven, CT: Yale University Press.

Lareau, Annette. 2003. *Unequal Childhoods: Class, Race, and Family Life.* Berkeley: University of California Press.

Lawrence, Denis. 2006. *Enhancing Self-Esteem in the Classroom,* 3rd ed. London: Paul Chapman.

Lee, Cecilia. 2005. "Delaware Diplomas: Back to Square One." *Wilmington* [DE] *News Journal,* May 22.

Leverence, John. 1997. *And the Winner Is . . . : Using Awards Programs to Promote Your Company and Encourage Your Employees.* Santa Monica, CA: Merritt.

Love Is Murder. 2009. "Lovey Awards." www.loveismurder.net/awards (retrieved June 24, 2009).

Luebke, Neil R. 2001. *A Century of Scholarship: The One-Hundred-Year History of the Honor Society of Phi Kappa Phi.* Phoenix, AZ: Heritage.

Malice Domestic. 2009. "Agatha Awards." www.malicedomestic.org (retrieved June 24, 2009).

Mansfield, Harvey C. 2001. "Grade Inflation: It's Time to Face the Facts." *Chronicle of Higher Education,* April 6, B24.

Marine, Michael M. 2004. "The Army-Navy 'Game': Understanding the Medal Gap between United States Naval Aviation and the United States Army Air Forces during World War II." *Journal of the Orders and Medals Society of America* 55 (May): 23–26.

Marquardt, Patrick D. 2009. "The Effect of Accountability-Based Testing on College-Bound Students." Unpublished paper, George Mason University.

Marshall, S. L. A. 1953. "Do the Real Heroes Get the Medal of Honor?" *Colliers,* February 21, 13–15.

Mathews, Jay. 1997. "A Farewell to Traditional Valedictorians." *Washington Post,* June 26, J1.

———. 2007. "Who Needs Honors Courses? Try Everyone." *Washington Post,* July 17, A19.

McCormick, Alexander C. 2007. "Hidden in Plain View." *Inside Higher Ed* (May 5). www.insidehighered.com (retrieved May 10, 2007).

McInerney, Fran. 2006. "Heroic Frames: Discursive Constructions Around the Requested Death Movement in Australia in the Late-1990s." *Social Science and Medicine* 62: 654–67.

McKinsey & Company. 2009. *"And the Winner Is . . . ": Capturing the Promise of Philanthropic Prizes.* Sydney, Australia: McKinsey & Company.

McPhedran, Ian. 2003. "Secret Heroes." *Daily Telegraph* [Sydney, Australia], December 11, 1.

Meredith, Marc. 2004. "Why Do Universities Compete in the Ratings Game? An Empirical Analysis of the Effects of the *U.S. News and World Report* College Rankings." *Research in Higher Education* 45: 443–61.

Messner, Michael A. 2009. *It's All for the Kids: Gender, Families, and Youth Sports.* Berkeley: University of California Press.

Meyer, Karl E. 1990. "The Editorial Notebook: Trenchcoats, Then and Now." *New York Times,* June 24, 20.

Minnesota Veterinary Medical Association. 2009. "Minnesota Animal Hall of Fame." www.mvma.org/hall_of_fame.asp (retrieved June 25, 2009).

Monahan, Brian A. 2010. *The Shock of the News: Media Coverage and the Making of 9/11.* New York: New York University Press.

Morse, Robert, and Sam Flanigan. 2009. "Law School Rankings Methodology." *USNews.com* (April 22). www.usnews.com (retrieved July 18, 2009).

Motion Picture Association of America. 2009. "Film Ratings." www.mpaa.org/FilmRatings.asp (retrieved July 8, 2009).

Mugno, Charles V. 1994. "Maintaining the Quality of Our Military Awards System." *Marine Corps Gazette* 78 (March): 77–83.

Myers, Michele Tolela. 2007. "The Cost of Bucking College Rankings." *Washington Post,* March 11, B7.

My Hero Project. 2009. "My Hero." www.myhero.com (retrieved May 31, 2009).

Mystery Ink. 2009. "Gumshoe Awards." www.mysteryinkonline.com (retrieved June 24, 2009).

Mystery Readers International. 2009. "McCavity Awards." www.mysteryreaders.org (retrieved June 24, 2009).

Mystery Writers of America. 2009. "Awards and Programs." www.mysterywriters.org (retrieved June 24, 2009).

National Association of Elementary School Principals. 2008. "National Elementary Honor Society™ Launched by Secondary and Elementary School Principals Associations." Press release, April 4. www.naesp.org (retrieved February 7, 2010).

National Center for Education Statistics. 2008. *Digest of Education Statistics: 2007.* Washington: U.S. Department of Education. http://nces.ed.gov/programs/digest/d07 (retrieved April 23, 2009).

National Commission on Excellence in Education. 1983. *A Nation at Risk: The Imperative for Educational Reform.* Washington, DC: Government Printing Office.

New York Times. 1971. "Veterans Discard Medals in War Protest at Capitol." April 24, 1.

———. 2008. "Who Spread False Tales of Heroism" [editorial]. July 16, 18.

Newman, A. S. 1967. "Who Gets the Combat Decorations?" *Army* 17 (January): 30–31.

Ngah, Zainab Awang. 1995. "Literary Prizes in Malaysia: Awards, Organizers and Authors." *Information Development* 11: 105–10.

Noguera, Pedro. 2003. *City Schools and the American Dream: Reclaiming the Promise of Public Education.* New York: Teachers College Press.

Nyberg, Amy Kiste. 1998. *Seal of Approval: The History of the Comics Code.* Jackson: University Press of Mississippi.

Nyhan, David. 1997. "A Long-Delayed Lesson in Wartime Courage— and Peacetime Racism." *Boston Globe,* January 17, A19.

Omnimystery. 2009. "Mystery Book Awards." www.omnimystery.com (retrieved June 24, 2009).

Oxford English Dictionary. 2009. "Star" and "Superstar." OED Online (retrieved August 21, 2009).

Packard, Vance. 1959. *The Status Seekers.* New York: David McKay.

ParaNormalRomance Groups. 2009. "P.E.A.R.L.: Paranormal Excellence Award for Romantic Literature." www.paranormalromance.org/PNRpearl (retrieved June 24, 2009).

Perez-Pena, Richard. 2007. "Pataki's Tours for 9/11 Silence Usual Critics." *New York Times,* September 7, B1.

Peterson, Iver. 1972. "Flunking Is Harder as College Grades Rise Rapidly." *New York Times,* March 13, 1, 21.

Peterson, Karyn M. 2007. "Hometown Heroes: Fire, Police and Rescue Toys Play Important Roles." *Playthings* (January) www.playthings.com/article/CA6405858.html (retrieved May 31, 2009).

Pew Research Center. 2006. *Are We Happy Yet?* Pew Research Center, Social Trends Report. http://pewresearch.org/assets/social/pdf/AreWeHappyYet (retrieved October 10, 2008).

Plummer, Deborah. 2007. *Self-Esteem Games for Children.* Philadelphia: Jessica Kingsley.

Porpora, Douglas V. 1996. "Personal Heroes, Religion, and Transcendental Metanarratives." *Sociological Forum* 11: 209–29.

Private Eye Writers of America. 2009. "The Shamus Awards." www.thrillingdetective.com/trivia/triv72 (retrieved June 24, 2009).

Purina (Canada). 2009. "Purina Animal Hall of Fame." www.purina.ca/about/halloffame (retrieved June 25, 2009).

Putnam, Robert D. 2000. *Bowling Alone: The Collapse and Revival of American Community.* New York: Simon & Schuster.

Radford, Peter. 2005. "Lifting the Spirits of the Nation: British Boxers and the Emergence of the National Sporting Hero at the Time of the Napoleonic Wars." *Identities* 12: 249–70.

Raglan, Lord [FitzRoy Richard Somerset Raglan, baron]. 1936. *The Hero: A Study in Tradition, Myth, and Drama.* London: Methuen.

Ravitch, Diane. 2000. *Left Back: A Century of Failed School Reforms.* New York: Simon & Schuster.

Reagan, Ronald. 1981. "First Inaugural Address." Miller Center for Public Affairs. http://millercenter.org (retrieved November 27, 2009).

Renold, Evelyn. 1975. "The Contemporary Movie Rating System in America." Pp. 76–97 in *Sexuality in the Movies,* edited by Thomas R. Atkins. Bloomington: Indiana University Press.

Reynolds, John, Michael Stewart, Ryan MacDonald, and Lacey Sischo. 2006. "Have Adolescents Become Too Ambitious? High School Seniors' Education and Occupational Plans, 1976 to 2000." *Social Problems* 53: 186–206.

Riding, Alan. 2005. "Arts Prizes Just for Women: Still Useful Spotlights in a Post-Feminist World." *New York Times,* June 23, E7.

Riemer, Jeffrey W. 1998. "Durkheim's 'Heroic Suicide' in Military Combat." *Armed Forces and Society* 25: 103–20.

Riesman, David. 1950. *The Lonely Crowd: A Study of the Changing American Character.* New Haven, CT: Yale University Press.

Roberts, Selena. 2002. "Figure Skating; Some Judges Say Overrule in the Pairs Is Not Justice." *New York Times,* February 18, D1.

Robin, Ron. 2004. *Scandals and Scoundrels: Seven Cases That Shook the Academy.* Berkeley: University of California Press.

Romance Writers of America. 2009. "National Awards and Contests." www.rwanational.org/cs/contests_and_awards (retrieved June 24, 2009).

Romano, Lois. 2004. "Keen Focus on Lt. Kerry's Four Months Under Fire." *Washington Post*, April 23, A1.

Romantic Novelists' Association. 2009. "RNA Awards." www.ma-uk .org (retrieved June 24, 2009).

Romantic Times. 2009. "Awards." www.romantictimes.com/books_awards (retrieved June 24, 2009; now www.rtbookreviews.com/rt-awards/ nominees-and-winners).

Rosenberg, Bernard, and David Manning White, eds. 1957. *Mass Culture: The Popular Arts in America.* New York: Free Press.

Rosenfeld, Richard, and Janet L. Lauritsen. 2008. "The Most Dangerous Crime Rankings." *Contexts* 7 (February): 66–67.

Rotten Tomatoes. 2009. www.rottentomatoes.com (retrieved June 9, 2009).

Rubin, Richard. 1997. "The Mall of Fame." *Atlantic Monthly* 280 (July): 14–16.

Rutenberg, Jim. 2004. "Delegates Mock Kerry's Wounds, Angering Veterans." *Washington Times* (September 1): 8.

Salisbury, Harrison. 1958. *The Shook-Up Generation.* New York: Harper.

Sarkesian, Sam C. 1975. *The Professional Army Officer in a Changing Society.* Chicago: Nelson-Hall.

Sauder, Michael. 2006. "Third Parties and Status Position: How the Characteristics of Status Systems Matter." *Theoretical Sociology* 35: 299–321.

Sauder, Michael, and Gary Alan Fine. 2008. "Arbiters, Entrepreneurs, and the Shaping of Business School Reputations." *Sociological Forum* 23: 699–723.

Sauder, Michael, and Ryon Lancaster. 2006. "Do Rankings Matter? The Effects of *U.S. News & World Report* Rankings on the Admissions Process of Law Schools." *Law and Society Review* 40: 105–34.

Schemo, Diana Jean. 2009. "Congratulations! You Are Nominated. It's an Honor. (It's a Sales Pitch.)" *New York Times (Education Life),* April 19, 16–19.

Schuman, Howard, Barry Schwartz, and Hannah D'Arcy. 2005. "Elite Revisionists and Popular Beliefs: Christopher Columbus, Hero or Villain?" *Public Opinion Quarterly* 69: 2–29.

Schwartz, Barry. 2009. "Collective Forgetting and the Symbolic Power of Oneness: The Strange Apotheosis of Rosa Parks." *Social Psychology Quarterly* 72: 123–42.

Seale, Clive. 1995. "Heroic Death." *Sociology* 29: 597–613.

———. 2002. "Cancer Heroics: A Study of News Reports with Particular Reference to Gender." *Sociology* 36: 107–26.

Short Mystery Fiction Society. 2009. "Short Mystery Fiction Society Derringer Awards." www.shortmystery.net (retrieved June 24, 2009).

Shulleeta, Brandon. 2008. "Want That Advanced Diploma? Try Charlottesville's New Math." *Daily Progress* [Charlottesville, VA], August 22. (retrieved through OneFile, April 13, 2009).

Slater, Philip. 1970. *The Pursuit of Loneliness: American Culture at the Breaking Point.* Boston: Beacon.

Sontag, Susan. 1978. *Illness as Metaphor.* New York: Farrar, Straus and Giroux.

Spencer, Martin E. 1979. "On the Conflict of Social Philosophies in Higher Education." *American Sociologist* 14: 246–51.

Stone, Andrea. 1999. "A Question of Honors." *USA Today,* November 11, 1A.

Stout, David. 2000. "Top Honors Come Belatedly for Asian-American Soldiers." *New York Times,* June 22, A18.

Strauss, Anselm. 1982. "Social Worlds and Legitimation Processes." *Studies in Symbolic Interaction* 4: 171–90

———. 1984. "Social Worlds and Their Segmentation Processes." *Studies in Symbolic Interaction* 5: 123–39.

Street, John. 2005. "'Showbusiness of a Serious Kind': A Cultural Politics of the Arts Prize." *Media, Culture and Society* 27: 819–40.

Sutherland, Amy. 2003. *Cookoff: Recipe Fever in America.* New York: Penguin.

Talbot, Margaret. 2005. "Best in Class." *New Yorker,* June 6, 38–41.

Thomson, Desson. 2008. "What the Oscar Drama Needs Is Some Comic Relief." *Washington Post,* February 17, M3.

Tilly, Charles. 2008. *Credit and Blame.* Princeton, NJ: Princeton University Press.

Todd, Richard. 1996. *Consuming Fictions: The Booker Prize and Fiction in Britain Today.* London: Bloomsbury.

Toffler, Alvin. 1970. *Future Shock.* New York: Random House.

Trice, Harrison M. 1985. "Rites and Ceremonials in Organizational Cultures." *Research in the Sociology of Organizations* 4: 221–70.

Tuchman, Gaye. 2009. *Wannabe U: Inside the Corporate University.* Chicago: University of Chicago Press.

Tugend, Alina. 2007. "The Guy Who Picks the Best Places to Live." *New York Times,* May 6, section 11, 1.

Turner, Bryan S. 1988. *Status.* Minneapolis: University of Minnesota Press.

Turow, Joseph. 1997. *Breaking Up America: Advertisers and the New Media World.* Chicago: University of Chicago Press.

Twenge, Jean M., and W. Keith Campbell. 2008. "Increases in Positive Self-Views Among High School Students." *Psychological Science* 19: 1082–86.

————. 2009. *The Narcissism Epidemic: Living in the Age of Entitlement.* New York: Free Press.

Unruh, David R. 1980. "The Nature of Social Worlds." *Pacific Sociological Review* 23: 271–96.

U.S. News & World Report. 2008. "Undergraduate Ranking Criteria and Weights." (August 21). www.usnews.com/articles/education/best-colleges/2008/08/21 (retrieved July 16, 2009).

Ward, Steven. 1996. "Filling the World with Self-Esteem: A Social History of Truth-Making." *Canadian Journal of Sociology* 21: 1–23.

Warren, John Robert, Eric Grodsky, and Jennifer C. Lee. 2008. "State High School Exit Examinations and Postsecondary Labor Market Outcomes." *Sociology of Education* 81: 77–107.

Washington Monthly. 2006. "The Washington Monthly College Rankings." (September). www.washingtonmonthly.com (retrieved July 21, 2009).

———. 2007. "A Note on Methodology." (June). www.washington monthly.com (retrieved July 21, 2009).

Washington Times. 2003. "Noble and Knave of the Year" [editorial]. January 4, A11.

Weber, Max. 1946. "Class, Status, and Party." Pp. 180–95 in *From Max Weber,* edited by H.H. Gerth and C. Wright Mills. New York: Oxford University Press [essay orig. pub. 1922].

Weiss, Michael J. 2000. *The Clustered World: How We Live, What We Buy, and What It All Means about Who We Are.* Boston: Little, Brown.

Wieting, Stephen G. 2000. "Twilight of the Hero in the Tour de France." *International Review for the Sociology of Sport* 35: 348–63.

Williams, Clint. 2002. "Civil War Re-enactors Divided—Over Style." *Atlanta Journal-Constitution,* September 21, 5H.

Wolfe, Tom. 1968. *The Pump House Gang.* New York: Farrar, Straus and Giroux.

Wolfe Pack. 2009. www.nerowolfe.org (retrieved June 24, 2009).

Wylie, Philip. 1942. *Generation of Vipers.* New York: Rinehart.

Zangen, Britta. 2003. "Women as Readers, Writers, and Judges: The Controversy about the Orange Prize for Fiction." *Women's Studies* 32: 281–99.

Zaslow, Jeffrey. 2007. "Most Praised Generation Craves Kudos at the Office." *Wall Street Journal Online,* April 23. www.careerjournal.com (retrieved May 10, 2007).

Zuckerman, Harriet. 1977. *Scientific Elite: Nobel Laureates in the United States.* New York: Free Press.

———. 1992. "The Proliferation of Prizes: Nobel Complements and Nobel Surrogates in the Reward System of Science." *Theoretical Medicine* 13: 217–31.

INDEX

Stat-Spotting
A Field Guide to Identifying Dubious Data

"If you ever scan the newspaper, watch the TV news, or surf the blogs, you should read this charming book. If you're a journalist, read it twice." —**James M. Jasper**

$21.95 cloth 978-0-520-25746-7 (W)

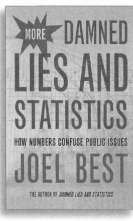

More Damned Lies and Statistics
How Numbers Confuse Public Issues

"Best provides us with another telling compendium of misleading statistics about a variety of topical issues. His approach to explicating them is lucid, instructive, and quite engaging." —**John Allen Paulos, author of *Innumeracy***

$21.95 cloth 978-0-520-23830-5 (W)

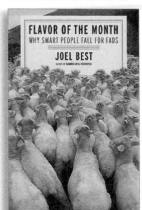

Flavor of the Month
Why Smart People Fall for Fads

"'A clearly written and overdue overview and analysis of the subject. Besides, there may be just enough to make this book on fads into one: It offers a simple step-by-step explanation with catchy names that will entertain business and academic conventions for the usual year."

—*San Francisco Chronicle*

$23.95 cloth 978-0-520-24626-3 (W)